The
Lira da Braccio

PUBLICATIONS OF THE EARLY MUSIC INSTITUTE
THOMAS BINKLEY, GENERAL EDITOR

Detail of the painting
Madonna and Child with Saints
by
Cima Giovanni Battista da Conegliano, ca. 1510
Galleria Nazionale, Parma
(see B-9, p. 21)

The Lira da Braccio

STERLING SCOTT JONES

INDIANA UNIVERSITY PRESS

BLOOMINGTON & INDIANAPOLIS

© 1995 by Sterling Scott Jones

Manufactured in the United States of America

Library of Congress Cataloging-in-Publication Data

Jones, Sterling Scott.
    The lira da braccio / Sterling Scott Jones.
        p. cm. -- (Publications of the Early Music Institute)
    Includes bibliographical references.
    ISBN 0-253-20911-0 (paper : alk. paper)
    1. Lira da braccio. I. Title. II. Series.
    ML927.L57J66 1995
    787.6--dc20   94-9019

    1 2 3 4 5 00 99 98 97 96 95   MN

Contents

Illustrations

Preface

Although the early music movement has produced many excellent players of the medieval fiddle over the last few decades, there has been relatively little interest in delving into its successor, the lira da braccio. There are now many proficient performers on baroque violin and viola, but few have been curious about the instrument which had its beginnings along with them. My own interest took wing after obtaining two such instruments: a copy of the Giovanni Maria lira da braccio in the Ashmolean Museum in Oxford made by Fabrizio Reginato (Fonte Alto, Italy) in 1976, followed by a copy of a larger instrument located in the Music Conservatory Museum in Brussels by an anonymous Italian maker, made by Fabrizio Reginato in 1978.

The very lack of concrete knowledge about the lira da braccio and its technical difficulties are a direct challenge in discovering how to make use of the instrument in 16th-century music. The lira da braccio was an obvious attempt at making use of bowed strings chordally without sacrificing melodic possibilities. My first reaction was a feeling of being limited by the almost flat bridge, but after finding my way about I soon discovered a broad spectrum of chordal possibilities hardly possible on any other bowed string instrument. These I have tried to organize in Chapters 5 and 6 of this presentation, including various pieces showing a few ways in which I have made use of the lira da braccio. I have devised a type of fingering tablature to aid in finding chords, which more often than not involves unexpected fingering and string combinations because of the unique tuning of the instrument.

Chapters 1 through 4 include a short history of the lira da braccio, which I felt would be useful as background, and observations of over a hundred contemporary pictorial representations of the instrument and of the few surviving examples which exist in museums and collections.

It is hoped that this might provide stimulus for string players and makers of string instruments to investigate further the uses of the lira da braccio in performance.

My thanks to Dr. Margaret Downie Banks, Curator of The Shrine to Music Museum at the University of South Dakota, for providing me with information about the lira da braccio in its collection; to Uta Henning in Ludwigsburg, Germany, for the use of her music instrument picture collection; and to Vladimir Ivanoff for providing me with photocopies of the appropriate pages from the Pesaro Ms. My thanks also to the Kusthistorisches Museum in Vienna, the Galleria Nazionale in Parma, and the Biblioteca Comunale Oliveriana in Pesaro for their permission to use photo reproductions; and to the Zentralinstitut für Kunstgeschichte in Munich for their help, and use of their library.

Sterling Scott Jones
Munich, Germany

The Lira da Braccio

1
A Short History of the Lira da Braccio

In searching for the origins of the violin, specialists in the field claimed to have discovered that the lira da braccio was an important key to the issue. The instrument which showed basic characteristics of the medieval fiddle also showed constructional features of the violin long before the violin came into its own; consequently they believed it to be the missing link between the fiddle and the violin. The more plausible theory is that both the lira da braccio and the violin had their beginnings at about the same time, providing witness to the fact that much experimentation was taking place with new instruments.[1] The lira da braccio appeared at the end of the 15th century, florished in the first third of the 16th century, continued to appear throughout the rest of the century, but disappeared early in the 17th century. Lira da braccio characteristics common to the late medieval fiddle were the spade- or leaf-shaped pegbox, the vertical pegs, in early instances the guitar-shaped body, the open strings along the side of the fingerboard, and the use of octaves in the tuning pattern.[2] It is difficult to distinguish between a fiddle and a lira da braccio in late 15th-century iconography. Features common to the violin were the four-cornered body shape of the lira da braccio, one of its most usual forms, and, except for the octave patterns, by the tuning (see below).[3]

Sources, Tunings, and String Set-up

Even though the lira da braccio is one of the most frequently depicted instruments in paintings and drawings of the Italian Renaissance, particularly during the early 16th century--the instrument seems to have been exclusively Italian--it is one which we know least about. This is because so few instruments have survived and because no written music for the instrument has been found except for a short section added in 1540-45 to an earlier lute manuscript (Pesaro).[4] In this manuscript there are several charts in tablature showing notes, some chord positions, one short piece entitled "Romanescha" (which is, however, a setting of the passamezzo moderno), and a fragment of a "Pasamezo."[5] These are written in Italian tablature for a six-string instrument (or where in any case only six strings are used) tuned d-d'/g-g'-d'-a'.[6]

The lira da braccio usually had seven strings, five on the fingerboard and two open strings along the side. Lanfranco (1533)[7] gave a tuning for the instrument as d-d'/g-g'-d'-a'-e". Praetorius (1619)[8] gave the same tuning but with the top string tuned to a d" rather than e" which put the top two strings a fourth instead of a fifth apart. This was related to the medieval fiddle, where a similar tuning including fourths existed. Praetorius also illustrated the instrument with frets, which are rare in the pictorial evidence (ex. A-33). Even though seven-string instruments were the most frequent, as is the case with all surviving instruments still in their original state, other on-and-off-the-fingerboard combinations show up in the iconography such as 3+1, 4+1, 4+2, 5+1, 7+2, 8+1. However, in spite of clarity one cannot always be sure where artistic liberties have played a role, as, for example, in the Raphael representation of Apollo, where nine strings on a lira da braccio symbolize the nine Muses.[9] Generally strings are shown equidistant, but often the two off-the-fingerboard strings appear closer together. An instrument in the Brussels museum (see note 15) has the strings tuned to octaves close together, those being the two lowest on the fingerboard and the two off the fingerboard. Paintings and drawings show most bridges slightly rounded, but a few appear to be absolutely flat. Most bridges are shown placed low or below the sound holes close to the tail piece, a few are placed centrally, and fewer still are placed high between the sound holes.

Shapes and Characteristics

The most frequent lira da braccio body shape seen throughout the history of the instrument was with four corners, two on the upper bouts, two on the lower bouts, similar to the shape of

Type A

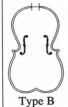
Type B

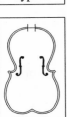
Type C

the violin (see type A). A unique feature of the lira da braccio was the indentation at the lower end of the body where the tail piece was attached. This can be observed on all extant instruments and on many of the instruments in pictures. It may have had symbolic connections with the shape of the female torso, as with the famous instrument (described below) by Giovanni d'Andrea located in the Vienna museum.[10] The constructional feature of the end indentation, although perhaps not originally intended for the purpose, facilitated holding very large instruments across the chest, with the end supported at the indentation by an upper part of the bow arm.[11] Most paintings and prints show the instrument placed on the shoulder or under the chin, in spite of some instruments appearing to be very large (see A-1, and A-5).

Another frequently encountered lira da braccio body shape was with two corners, usually one on each side of the lower bouts (see type B).[12] In drawings and paintings this shape appears almost entirely within the first third of the 16th century. The end indentation was also sometimes present with this shape, as with the two undated extant instruments believed to have originally been liras but later changed to violas.[13]

A third type, the one most closely related to the medieval fiddle, had no corners, and is described as the guitar shape (see type C). Again, almost all of the encountered pictorial evidence for this shape occur within the first third of the 16th century, with some dating from the end of the 15th century. No instruments of this type have survived. The indented end typical of the lira da braccio was not usual with this shape, nor was it typical of fiddles. One example found in the iconography dating from the first decade of the 16th century shows an oval body, a shape sometimes found on medieval fiddles as well (see type E).

Type E

A great variety can be seen in the shapes of sound holes on instruments in the iconography and on extant instruments (see examples). C-shaped sound holes facing inward were the most common type on the liras da braccio of all shapes up to about the middle of the 16th century and

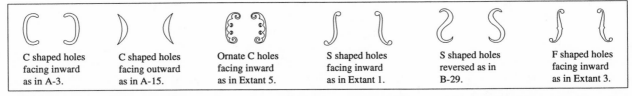

| C shaped holes facing inward as in A-3. | C shaped holes facing outward as in A-15. | Ornate C holes facing inward as in Extant 5. | S shaped holes facing inward as in Extant 1. | S shaped holes reversed as in B-29. | F shaped holes facing inward as in Extant 3. |

were typical of medieval fiddles as well. Some C-shaped holes are shown facing outward, and a few are quite ornate. A few S- or F-shaped sound holes began to appear on instruments early in the 16th century, but were seen more frequently during the second half of the century. No sound holes of this type are encountered on pictures of guitar-shaped instruments.

Extant Instruments

Of the few liras da braccio which have survived only two or three are unaltered. The earliest of these, by Giovanni d'Andrea (see note 10) dating from 1511, now in the Vienna museum, is also the most decorative. It is the maker's only known instrument. If we were to see the instrument in a drawing or painting from the 16th century we would assume it to be a product of the artist's imagination. The body of the instrument implies human forms with breasts on both front and back; and the back shows acanthus leaves and a mask superimposed on a female torso. The pegbox shows human faces on the front and on the closable back cover. Another fine instrument in its original state was made by Giovanni Maria da Brescia and is located in the Oxford Ashmolean Museum. It is not dated, and there is much speculation as to when this instrument was built. It is ornamented with inlaid designs on the front and sides of the pegbox.[14] A lira da braccio in the Brussels museum by an unknown maker also appears to be in its original condition.[15] Other generally known extant instruments no longer have their original necks, fingerboards, or pegboxes (see note 21).

A great variety of sizes can be observed when comparing extant instruments and those seen in iconographical material. There are too few surviving instruments to determine any average sizes. Only the above-mentioned few retain their original necks, the Giovanni d'Andrea instrument possibly even its original bridge. The others have been restored or changed to violas. Body length ranges from 38.7 cm, the size of a small viola, to 59 cm, larger than even a large viola. The Oxford instrument of Giovanni Maria has a string length of 32.3 cm (in the violin range), the Brussels instrument (no. 1443) one of about 36 cm, and the Vienna instrument by Giovanni d'Andrea of about 41 cm (a large viola size). If the large instruments used a normal seven-string tuning pattern, they were undoubtedly tuned to an alto range, a fifth lower.

Terminology and Application

Various names other than lira da braccio were used in the 16th century, the most frequent being *lira*[16] or *lira moderna*, the latter distinguishing it from the antique lyre from which it was supposedly derived. This derivation was of course erroneous, even though the instrument displayed some characteristics which might have been associated with the ancient Greek lyre, such as seven strings, two of which were not on the fingerboard. Other names were *lira da spalla* and *lira di sette corde*.[17] In the second half of the century liras da braccio were beginning to be called violas. In 1564 Vasari described an instrument played by an angel in a Carpaccio painting as *una lira ovvero viola*[18] (a lira or viola). At this time viols were usually referred to as violas with frets (Ganassi: *viola d'arco tastada*). In 1569 Massimo Troiano, an Italian composer and courtier, described the festivities which took place in Munich for the wedding of Wilhelm V of Bavaria and Renata of Lorraine the year before. Troiano mentions the names of viola da braccio players as well as the pieces in which violas were used, sometimes as many as six. Whether these included liras da braccio is open to question in light of the changing nomenclature.[19] In 1581 Vincenzo Galilei made the interesting comment that in the not too distant past the viola da braccio was called lira.[20] These comments raise some intriguing questions. Do they indicate that the lira da braccio was becoming obsolete? Were liras da braccio being changed into violas? Several of the extant liras da braccio were certainly changed into violas at some point.[21] Were *lironi* intended when *lira* instruments were called for, these being the bass counterparts to the lira da braccio?[22] The lirone was coming more into use by the middle of the century, and, with evidence of its use far into the 17th century, it outlasted the lira da braccio. We find the lira da braccio still being used during the latter part of the 16th century in *intermedia* accompanying madrigals along with other instruments; for example, in the famous Florentine *intermedia* of 1589, where liras were called for.[23] Francesco Rognoni still talked about the instrument in 1620 in his *Selva de Varii Pasaggi /Parte Seconda,* saying, however, that the instrument was little known (*la Lira da Brazzo poi, benche da pochi conosciuta*). An interesting added bit of information given by Rognoni is his comment that liras should use long bows (*la Lira in se stessa ama l'arco longo, aciò si possa lireggiare meglio*), a point sometimes but not always verified in the iconografical evidence.

The lira da braccio was portrayed very frequently in the 16th century as ideally fulfilling an improvisational accompanying role in the hands of antique mythological gods, poets, and musicians, such as Apollo, Orpheus, Homer, and King David (exx. A-1, A-15, A-28, A-34, B-14, C-8). This tells us much about the Renaissance musician's attitude toward the lira da braccio and its function. The poet-musicians of Italian courts used the instrument to accompany the singing of their recitations, narrative verses, and epics, imagining themselves to be emulating ancient Greek tradition (ex. C-10). Ganassi talks about the practice of singing basses accompanied by the lira.[24] Agostino Beccari's *Il sacrificio*, a theatrical piece first performed in Ferrara in 1554, is an example of this.[25] The recitatives for bass (only the vocal part survives) were sung by Andrea dalla Viola accompanying himself on a lira da braccio, the music being composed by his brother Alfonso. Inasmuch as such accompaniments were improvised it is understandable that no written music has survived for the instrument. (See pp. 94 and 97 for suggested accompaniments to the three strophes of this recitative.)

Many religious paintings showed angels with liras da braccio, always appearing singly, never in pairs, but sometimes together with several other instruments (exx. A-5, B-9, C-12, C-19). This was also true when the lira da braccio appeared in secular surroundings (exx. A-19, C-11). In religious and allegorical paintings performers were angels or Muses, most often shown as females, in contrast to mythological subjects, where they were invariably male. One painting shows a single lira da braccio player performing before the enthroned Madonna with no other instruments present, indicating the high esteem in which the instrument was held.[26] One can only conjecture as to what sort of music this player might have been performing. In religious invironments the lira da braccio was most likely used to accompany Latin chants and psalms, as well as laude, these being hymns of praise in the Italian language. This usage may well reflect the beginnings of harmonized chant accompaniments still heard in Roman Catholic and Anglican Churches today.

Poet-musicians of the Italian courts in some cases sang in a range below the lira da braccio accompaniments, playing the instrument themselves, as in the dalla Viola recitative. The accompaniment was thus in a higher range than the sung part, which fulfilled the role of the bass line. The lira da braccio is incapable of playing a bass line; because of its unique tuning chords are often only possible in inverted positions.[27] It is interesting to note that the lira da braccio appeared in order to utilize the new chordal harmonies of the time, as seen in the three- and four-voiced treatment of the *sonetti, strambotti,* and *frottole* forms which developed in the social atmosphere of the courts at Verona, Padua, Mantua, and Venice of the early 16th century. It is no coincidence that it is in this north Italian area that we find the lira da braccio most extensively documented in pictures and drawings, and that all extant instruments originate.[28] How the lira da braccio was employed in the *frottole* one can only guess, since this music usually provided a treble melody with accompaniment rather than a bass melody with accompaniment, a performance practice documented for the lira da braccio. This placement of melody on top and harmonies below was sympathetic to the capabilities of the lira da braccio, which was able to bow only the top one or two strings separately and the lower strings in groups, depending on the curvature of the bridge and the spacing of the strings.[29] The one surviving complete piece for lira da braccio, the Romanesca in the Pesaro Ms. has chords of the bass pattern, some in inverted positions, interspersed with melody on the top strings. Another bit of interesting evidence is provided by a piece written by Biagio Marini in the early 17th century: *Capriccio per Sonare il Violino con tre corde à modo di Lira* (Capriccio for violin with three strings used in the style of the lira). The composer notes that the two lower strings need to be close together (*bisogna che le due corde grosse sijno vicine*).[30] Accompanied by a basso continuo, the violin plays chordal sections set off by florid passages on the top string. The piece was written at a time when the lira da braccio was certainly already out of fashion, but its sounds were still remembered.

Notes

1. For more on the relationship of the lira da braccio and the violin, see the earliest study on the lira da braccio, by Hajdecki, *Italienische Lira da Braccio.*

2. Documented on fiddles in the late 13th century in tunings given by Jerome of Moravia (see Page "Jerome of Moravia on the *rubeba* and *viella,*" *Galpin Society Journal,* 32, 1979, pp. 77-95), and in pictorial evidence such as the *Cantigas de Santa Maria* manuscript miniatures of fiddles.

3. To establish the identity of a lira da braccio as opposed to a fiddle or a viola da braccio in the iconographical sources the following characteristics were looked for: a leaf- or spade-shaped pegbox as opposed to a scroll type, four or five strings on the fingerboard and one or two strings along the side of the fingerboard, the body shape--in particular the indentation at the bottom end by the tailpiece, the less-rounded features of the bridge, and general dating of the material. In many instances, however, not all of these characteristics present themselves, making identification with certainty almost impossible.

4. Pesaro, Biblioteca Oliveriana (1144, olim 1193), studied in Rubsamen, "Earliest French Lute Tablature," in Ivanoff, *Das Pesaro-Manuscript,* and Ivanoff, *Eine Zentrale Quelle der Frühen Italienischen Lautenpraxis.* The section dealing with lira da braccio also appears in Brown, "Florentine Intermedii."

5. A number of pages from the lira da braccio section are unfortunately missing; they would have provided several more pieces for the instrument. See Ivanoff, *Das Pesaro-Manuscript,* p. 116.

6. In giving all the notes for the lira da braccio on a six-line tablature, the Pesaro Ms. adds the top notes for a seven-string instrument by means of a seventh ledger line. The tablature differs from Italian lute tablature inasmuch as only diatonic steps are indicated with numbers 1 to 4, resulting in no indication of raised or lowered accidentals except for an occasional use of a rather imprecise x. Therefore the tablature is actually a fingering chart with the numbers 1 to 4 indicating the four fingers. Written diagonally across the bottom of p. 175 of the Ms. is a table with solmization and numbers under the title *Aria Romana*. For an interpretation of this table see Appendix Commentary, p. 108.

7. Giovanni Maria Lanfanco, *Scintille di Musica* (Brescia, 1533).

8. Michael Praetorius, *De Organographia* (Wolfenbüttel, 1619).

9. Fresco: *Parnassus*, ca. 1511, Stanza della Segnatura, Vatican, Rome (see ex. B-14).

10. See Schlosser, *Sammlung*, catalog no. 94. The instrument is pictured in innumerable books on music and instruments. See below, pp. 11, 55, 56. In addition to the information about this instrument appearing on p. 11, I am grateful to Dr. Peter Klein of the University of Hamburg for the following interesting details. The table of the instrument is in three sections. The treble side has a piece of wood with 117 annual rings, and a smaller piece with 56 rings. The wood on the bass side of the table has 195 rings. The youngest ring on the treble side dates from the year 1504, the youngest ring on the bass side, from 1500. The instrument was built in 1511, thus indicating the use seasoned wood of at least seven years.

11. See ex. A-34, a painting by Jusepe Ribera (1588-1652) of Homer showing a lira da braccio held in this position. Ex. C-19, a fresco on the ceiling of the church of Santa Maria dei Miracoli in Saronno, Italy, gives evidence that lira da braccio type instruments were also played between the knees in "gamba" position. This, however, seems to be an isolated example.

12. For the relationship of this shape with that of a horse's skull see Winternitz, *Leonardo,* pp. 39-72. Ex. B-10 shows a rare example of two corners on the upper bouts.

13. See Boyden, *Catalogue*, no. D. 2: 2, and Mahillon, *Catalogue,* no. 1415. For questionable datings of these instruments, see Witten, "Apollo," p. 26.

14. Ashmolean Museum, Oxford, catalog no. D. 4: 1. For questionable dating from 1525 to 1575 see Boyden, *Catalogue*, pp. 15-16, and Witten, "Apollo," p. 46.

15. Brussels Music Conservatory Museum, Mahillon catalog no. 1443. There are noticable marks on the fingerboard indicating the use of frets at some time.

16. Giovanni Maria Lanfranco, *Scintille di Musica* (1533); and Pietro Cerone, *El Melopeo y Maestro* (1613).

17. Sylvestro Ganassi, *Regola Rubertina* (Venice, 1542), Section II, chapter 16.

18. Giorgio Vasari, *Le Vite,* (Milan, 1564). The painting is Carpaccio's *Presentation in the Temple* (Accademia, Venice). See ex. B-12.

19. *Dialoghi di Massimo Troiano* (Venice, 1569), facsimile and German translation by H. Leuchtmann, *Die Münchner Fürstenhochzeit von 1568* (Munich-Salzburg, 1980). String players mentioned by Troiano had Italian names (Antonio, Batista, and Aniballi Morari; Cerbonio Besutio, Lucio Terzo, Christoforo da Cremona) and were undoubtedly familiar with lira da braccio instruments, but none were shown in pictures of the Munich court orchestra such as the 1560 miniature by Hans Mielich, or the title page to the Lasso *Cantionum, quas mutetas vocant, opus novum* (Munich: Berg, 1573).

20. Vincenzo Galilei, *Dialogo della musica antica et della moderna* (Florence, 1581), p. 147, *viola da braccio, detta da non molti anni indietro lira.*

21. A Gasparo da Salò lira-viola dated 1561 in the Ashmolean Museum, Oxford (Boyden, *Catalogue*, no, D. 2: 2), a lira-viola in the Music Conservatory Museum, Brussels (Mahillon, *Catalogue*, catalog no. 1415), and a lira-viola instrument by Ventura Linarol dated 1580 in the Kunsthistorisches Museum, Vienna (Schlosser, catalogue no. C. 108) are examples. Other instruments which have since been restored to their lira da braccio forms include Berlin Instrument Museum no. 2578, by an unknown maker (see Sachs, *Sammlung,* p. 137, and Munrow, *Musikinstrumente,* p. 136), the Ventura Linarol instrument in the Heyer collection (see Kinsky, *Katalog,* pp. 414-15) now in Leipzig, an instrument at the London Royal College of Music, catalog no. 52 (see Baines, *Musical*

Instruments, nos. 5-6), and a lira da braccio by Francesco Linarol at the Shrine to Music Museum (no. 4203), Vermillion, South Dakota, U.S.A. (formerly in the W. E. Hill and Sons collection).

22. The lirone was a fretted instrument played between the knees. It had from nine to fourteen strings tuned in ascending fifths and descending fourths with two off-the-fingerboard strings tuned in octaves (G-g / c-c'-g-d'-a-e'-b-f♯'-c♯', Cerreto, *Prattica musica*, 1601).

23. Brown, "Florentine Intermedii," discusses how the lira da braccio was most likely used in *intermedio* ensembles in combination with other instruments, such as violin and lirone.

24. Ganassi, *Lettione seconda* (1543), Chapter 16: *prattica del dire i bassi accompagnado con il suon della Lyra*. Ganassi mentions that he intended to write more about the playing techniques of the instrument, but this unfortunately never materialized. Perhaps he realized that the lira da braccio was not as popular as it had been earlier in the century.

25. Biblioteca Nazionale, Florence (E-6-6-46). The work was performed on February 11 and March 4, 1554 in the palace of Don Francesco da Este, the first time before Duke Ercole II. It contains a sacrificial scene in which an invocation to Pan is sung and answered by brief calls from a chorus. The preface to the work states: *Fece la musica M. Alfonso dalla Viuola. Rappresentò il Sacerdote con la lira M. Andrea suo fratello* (music composed by Alfonso della Viola, the priest performed by his brother Andrea with the lira). According to Alfred Einstein, this is the first example of an accompanied recitative in drama. Printed in Einstein, *The Italian Madrigal*, I, pp. 301-302, and in Osthoff, *Theatergesang*, II, pp. 84-86: see musical example, p. 94, below.

26. The painting is *Sacra converazione*, by Palma Vecchio (ca. 1480-1528), San Zaccaria, Venice. See ex. B-28.

27. One painting shows the use of a metal ring on the thumb to stop a single off-the-fingerboard string, perhaps providing several more chords in root positions. It shows in any case an attempt at extending the capabilities of the instrument. The painting (before 1533) is the *Coronation of the Virgin* by Girolamo del Pacchia in the Chiesa di S. Spirito, Siena. See ex. C-18.

28. See Witten, "Apollo," 1975.

29. Disertori, in "Pratica e tecnica della lira da braccio" (1941), attempts to provide accompaniments to several *frottole* using an alto tuning for lira da braccio, a fifth lower than standard. He also tries to analyze fingering positions in order to determine the chords in paintings portraying lira da baccio players.

30. From Biagio Marini, *Sonate, Symphonie, Canzoni* (Venice, 1626). Excerpts published in Boyden, *History*, p. 131; and in Haas, *Aufführungspraxis*, p. 171. See below musical examples, pp. 105, 116.

Orpheus, *Istoria et favola di Orfeo*, Siena, ca. 1520.
(See A-15, p. 17)

2

Some Early Citations

Baldassare Castiglione, *Il Libro del Cortegiano* (Venice, 1528).
   "Good music means to me singing well and securely and in good style from the score; but much more still the singing to one's own *viola* [lira da braccio] accompaniment" (translated in Winternitz, *Symbolism*, p. 95). (*Bella musica . . . parmi il cantar bene a libro sicuramente, et con bella maniera: ma anchor molto più il cantare alla viola.*)

Giovanni Maria Lanfranco, *Sintille di Musica* (1533), pp. 136 ff.
   Gives tuning for the lira da bracio [d-d' / g-g'-d'-a'-e"] naming the strings from the bottom up as 1. basso grave, 2. basso acuto, 3. bordone grave, 4. bordone acuto, 5. tenore, 6. sottanella, 7. canto.

Silvestro Ganassi, *Regola Rubertina* (1543).
   Section I, Chapter 8, refers to a discovery in antique Rome where a figure is shown with a *viola d'arco*, "better identified as a *lira* or *lirone* and not *viola* or *violone.*" Section II, Chapter 16, speaks about *lira de sette corde* and how the gamba can be used in a similar manner. When performing a four- or five-part madrigal, in which four parts are played and the fifth is sung, one must obtain a long bow with less tension, tightening the bow with the fingers when fewer strings, or only one, are needed. In addition, the fingerboard, bridge, and tailpiece should not be too strongly arched so that chords can be comfortably managed. Mention is made of the practice of singing basses accompanied by the lira (*prattica del dire i bassi accompagnado con il suon della Lyra*). Ganassi says he intended to write more about the playing techniques of the instrument, but this unfortunately never materialized.

Document about cathedral music in Treviso, 1552. (See d'Alessi, "Maestri," p. 161.)
   An ensemble of six performing on lira and lirone (*compagnia di suonatori di lire e lironi*).

Giorgio Vasari, *Le Vite (*Milan, 1564).
   Le Vite III, 642. Identifies a lira da braccio played by an angel in the Carpaccio painting *Presentation in the Temple* as *una lira ovvero viola* (see ex. B-12), whereas an instrument in the *Sacre conversazione* painting of Fra Bartolommeo is simply indentified as a *lira* (see ex. B-21).
   Le Vite IV, 18, 28, 29, 498. Mentions the musical interests of Leonardo da Vinci and his "resolve to learn to play the lira da braccio, the nature of which, like himself, was noble and full of charm and with which he sang and improvised divinely" (*ma tosto si risolvè a imparere a suonare la lira, come quello che della natura aveva spirito elevatissimo e pieno di leggiadria, onde sopra quella cantò divinamente all'improviso*). In 1494 Leonardo was presented to the Duke at the court in Milan. The Duke also played the lira, and Leonardo's famous lira [da braccio?] is mentioned, "which he made himself, shaped like a horse's skull and decorated with silver, something odd and novel, a sonorous instrument with a penetrating sound with which he excelled over all the other musicians gathered there" (*quelle strumento ch'egle aveva di sua mano fabbricato d'argento gran parte in forme d'un teschio di cavallo, cosa bizarra et nuova, accioche l'armonia fosse con maggior tuba sonora di voce, laonde supero tutti i musici die quivi erano concorsi a sonare*). (For a discussion of this curious instrument, see Chapter 5 "The Mystery of the Skull Lyre," in Winternitz, *Leonardo*, p. 39). Praise is also given about Timoteo Viti, who played the lira da braccio and was the teacher of Raphael.

Vincenzo Galilei, *Dialogo della musica antica et della moderna* (Florence, 1581), pp. 130, 147.
Distinguishes between the Greek lyre, *lira antique* and the improvisation instrument of the Renaissance, *lira moderna*. Mentions that the viola da braccio was recently called *lira* (*viola da braccio, detta da non molti anni indietro lira*).

Pierio Valerianos, *Hieroglyphica* (Basel, 1567).
Pictures a pseudo-ancient Roman altar decorated with reliefs of a lira da braccio shown as an attribute of Mercury (see Winternitz, *Symbolism,* p. 26).

P. Abbate Picinelli, *Del Mondo Simbolico Ampliato*, Libro XXIII, Chapter V.
Speaks of *lire con l'archetto* as well as *lira toccata dal plettro* as instruments of antiquity.

Pietro Cerone, *Melopeo y Maestro* (1613), p. 1053.
Repeats the tuning given by Lanfranco (1533).

Michael Praetorius, *De Organographia* (Wolfenbüttel, 1619).
Repeats the tuning given by Lanfranco but with the top string tuned d".
Chapter XXIII: Mentions briefly that one can play three-part and other pieces (*tricinia und auch andere Sachen zuwege bringen kann*) on the small lira (*kleinen Lyra*).

Francesco Rognoni, *Selve de Varii Passagi/Parte Seconda* (Milan, 1620).
Mentions that the lira da braccio was little known (*la Lira da Brazzo poi, benche da pochi conosciuta*) and says that with the lira one should use a long bow (*la Lira in se stessa ama l'arco longo, aciò si possa lireggiare meglio*).

Marin Mersenne, *Harmonie Universelle* (1636). Livre IV, Propos. XIII.
States on Italian authority that one can play all types of music on the lira da braccio, that the instrument is most appropriate for singing narratives and sonnets and especially for sublime and lofty things, be it in the vernacular or in latin (*peut jouer toutes sortes de pièces de Musique dessus: que cet instrument est le plus propre de tous pour chanter des histoires & des sonnets, & particulièrement les choses sublimes & relevées tant en langue vulgaire qu'en Latin*).

Compendium of Lira da Braccio Shapes
(Sizes are not relative)

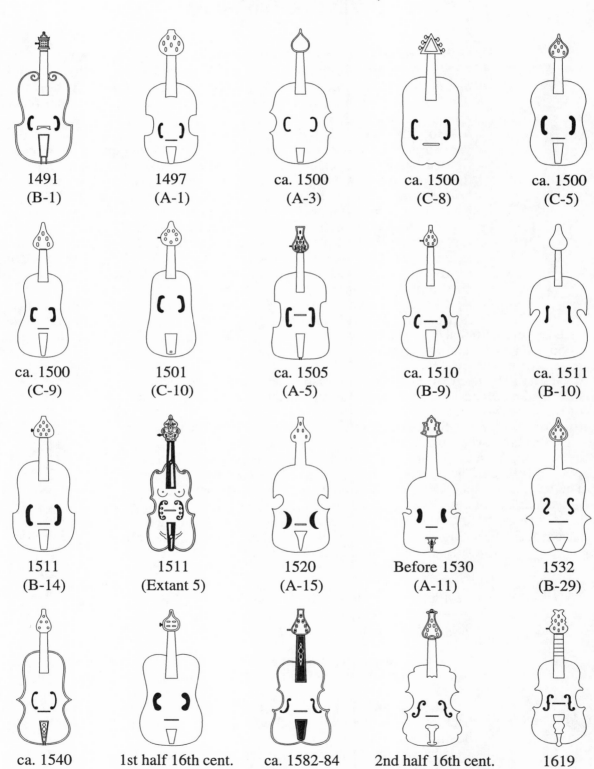

1491 (B-1)	1497 (A-1)	ca. 1500 (A-3)	ca. 1500 (C-8)	ca. 1500 (C-5)
ca. 1500 (C-9)	1501 (C-10)	ca. 1505 (A-5)	ca. 1510 (B-9)	ca. 1511 (B-10)
1511 (B-14)	1511 (Extant 5)	1520 (A-15)	Before 1530 (A-11)	1532 (B-29)
ca. 1540 (B-31)	1st half 16th cent. (C-18)	ca. 1582-84 (A-24)	2nd half 16th cent. (A-28)	1619 (A-33)

3
Extant Instruments

1. Lira da braccio by Giovanni Maria da Brescia, Venice, ca. 1525. Label of doubtful origin (Boyden; but Witten[1] believes it to be genuine, dating the instrument about 1575): Gioan maria bresiano / in Venetia [no date]. Located in the Hill Collection of the Ashmolean Museum (catalog no. D. 4: 1), Oxford.

Boyden[2] describes the instrument as being in perfect condition. The varnish is a golden-brown color with the ribs and one-piece back made of figured maple. The purfling is single and the pegbox has ornate designs on the front and sides. The pegbox, neck, and fingerboard are original; the bridge is not. The instrument has a sound post but no bass bar. The top and back of the instrument are in one piece, and there are no linings.[3]

Measurements in cm (Boyden): upper bouts: 18.7, center bouts: 13.5, lower bouts: 23.4, depth of sides: 3.4, length of fingerboard: 19.6, string length: 32.3, body length: 38.7, overall length: 64.7. There are five strings on a flat fingerboard, two strings off the fingerboard, seven pegs. The curved bridge is placed centrally between f-holes.

Pictured in Baines, *Musical Instruments*, nos. 2-3; in Baines, *Musical Instruments Through the Ages,* plate 10-a; in Boyden, *Catalogue*, plate 8, a-f; in Disertori, "Pratica," p. 152 (drawing); in Witten, "Apollo," p. 47, fig. 45; and in many other books on music and instruments.

2. Lira da braccio by an anonymous Italian maker of the 16th century. Located in the Music Conservatory Museum (Mahillon catalog III, no. 1443), Brussels. No label.

Five strings on a flat fingerboard, two strings off the fingerboard, seven pegs. The bridge is very low, being only 2.2 cm at the highest point, slightly curved, but probably not original. It is placed somewhat lower than center between F-holes. The neck, pegbox, and fingerboard appear to be original. The back is one piece with no perfling. There is no bass bar.[4]

Measurements in cm (Jones): upper bouts: 21, center bouts: 15, lower bouts: 25.5 (Parson[5] and Mahillon give 26), depth of sides: 3.6, length of fingerboard: 21.5, string length: app. 35.9, body length: 43.2, overall length: 69 (Mahillon gives 72). Disertori[6] gives the following measurements: lower bouts: 26, body length: 44, overall length: 72.[7]

Pictured in Disertori, "L'Arciviolatalira," p. 208 (drawing); the same drawing is in MGG, vol. 8, p. 935, and in Mahillon, *Catalogue*, vol. 3, p. 60.

3. Lira da braccio. Presumed false inscription on the inside of the back in ink: Joan Karlino Brescia 1452. Location: London, Royal College of Music, 52.

The instrument is similar to the Brussels lira da braccio no. 1443. The back is in one piece. The neck was at some time restored, and the fingerboard is also later.[8]

Measurements in cm (Baines): body length: 46, depth: 3.8, overall length: 72.5.

Pictured in Baines, *Musical Instruments*, nos. 5-6.

4. Lira da braccio by Francesco Linarol, Venice, 1563. Label: Francisci Linaroli Bergamensis / Venetiis 1563. Located at the Shrine to Music Museum (no. 4203), Vermillion, South Dakota, U.S.A. The instrument was formerly a part of the W. E. Hill and Sons collection of instruments.

The body of the instrument is entirely original except for the willow top-block and doubled edges on the table. The neck, leaf pegbox, fingerboard, and tailpiece are reproductions. The cedar table has an ornamental geometric purfling on the upper and lower flanks. The sound holes are S-shaped. The purfled back of the instrument is of pearwood. The pearwood ribs, which are carved to form a concave exterior shape, bear the Latin inscription in block letters: *Dum perare ovem transibit equus sursum reddit mellifluum sylba lo cante manu* (while the horse crosses the sheep up and down, the wood returns a mellifluous [sound]; hail the playing hand).[9] The varnish is of semi-transparent orange-brown color.

Measurements in cm (Monical): upper bouts: 24.7 (top), 24.35 (back); center bouts: 18.3 (top), 18.05 (back); lower bouts: 29.35 (top), 29.3 (back); body length: 50.55 (top), 51.2 (back). Rib height at top block: 3.6 (treble), 3.65 (bass); at upper corner: 3.85 (treble), 3.85 (bass); at center bouts: 4.0 (treble), 3.9 (bass); at lower corner: 3.8 (treble), 3.8 (bass); at bottom block: 3.75 (treble), 3.7 (bass). Table measure: 27.6. Vibrating string length (restoration): 43.9.

Pictured in Monical, *Shapes of the Baroque,* pp. 10-11; in Spicer, *The Shrine to Music Museum,* p. 12.

5. Lira da braccio by Joannes Andreas (Giovanni d'Andrea), Verona, 1511. Label: Joannes Andree. Veronen. / [adi 12?] . . uosto (agosto?) / 1511. Location: Kunsthistorisches Museum (Schlosser catalog no. 94), Vienna.

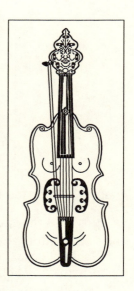

Schlosser[10] describes the instrument as being in excellent condition and the maker's only known instrument to date. The body of the instrument implies human forms with breasts on both front and back, the back showing acanthus leaves and a mask superimposed on a female torso. The pegbox shows human faces on the front and closable back cover. The intarsia fingerboard and tailpiece are made of ebony, ivory, brown wood, and bone dyed green. The bridge is possibly original. The varnish is a warm brown color on top and a dark reddish-brown on the bottom and sides. On the back side of the instrument is a small ivory label with the Greek inscription: DUPPS IAT // ROS ESTIN // ANQRWIIOIS / WAP (Song is the doctor to the pains of Man). Five strings on the fingerboard, two strings off the fingerboard, seven pegs, and a curved bridge (original?) placed centrally between ornate C-holes. No linings or bass bar. See also note 10 on p. 5.

Measurements in cm (Schlosser): maximum width upper bouts: 22.5, lower bouts: 27.5, depth of sides: 4.5, body length: 51.5, total length: 80.5.

Pictured in Baines, *Musical Instruments,* no. 1; in Clemencic, *Old Musical Instruments,* pp. 16-17; in Disertori, "L'Arciviolatalira," p. 208 (drawing); in Disertori, "Pratica," p. 151 (drawing); in *New Grove Dictionary,* vol. 11, p. 18; in MGG, vol. 8, p. 935 (drawing) and 937; in Schlosser, *Sammlung,* vol. 3, plate XX, no. 94; in Winternitz, *Leonardo,* p. 26; in Winternitz, *Musical Instruments,* p. 63; in Winternitz, *Symbolism,* plate 3l-g; in Witten, "Apollo," p. 30, fig. 25; and in many other books on music and instruments. See below, pp. 55, 56.

6. Lira (lirone) da braccio by Ventura di Francesco Linarolo, Venice, 1577. Located in the Heyer Collection (Kinsky catalog no. 780), Leipzig.[11] Written label: Ventura di Francesco / linarolo. In Venetia. 1577.

Kinsky[12] describes the back of the instrument as having a reddish-yellow varnish, being made out of two pieces of flaming maple. The sides curve inward. Both the top and the bottom have perfling. The tailpiece, neck, fingerboard, and pegbox are not original, but have been restored using the Tintoretto painting *Concert of Nymphs* as a model (see ex. A-24).

Because of its large size this instrument has been classified as a lirone by Disertori. It has, however, all the characteristics of the lira da braccio, such as the shape (indented end by tail piece) and the number of strings (five on the fingerboard, two off). Disertori suggests an alto tuning a fifth lower then normal. Although it would not be impossible to play the instrument under the chin, it is more likely that it was played in a cross-chest position, as seen in the painting *Homer* by Ribera (see ex. A-34) or in a "gamba" position, as seen in the fresco *Concert of Angels*, by Gaudenzio Ferrari (see ex. C-19).

Measurements in cm (Kinsky): upper bouts: 31.5, center bouts: 23, lower bouts: 40, length of fingerboard: 31, neck length: 16, depth of sides: 5.8, body length: 59, overall length: 92.

Pictured in Disertori, RMI 44, p. 208, as part of a drawing; the same drawing is in MGG, vol. 8, p. 935; pictured also in Kinsky, *Katalog*, p. 414, with description p. 415; in Kinsky, *Geschichte,* pp. 142-43; and in Witten, "Apollo," p. 47, fig. 46.

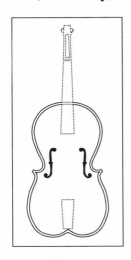

7. Lira-viola by Gasparo da Salò, Brescia, 1561.[13] Label: Gasparo da Salò, in Brescia / 1561. Located in the Hill Collection of the Ashmolean Museum (catalog no. D. 2: 2), Oxford.

Boyden[14] describes the instrument as having four strings, viola tuning, and characteristic lira da braccio indented base at the tailpiece. There are no middle bouts. The table of the instrument is made of latticed wood, golden brown in color, with F-holes. The two-pieced back and ribs are made of figured maple. Both front and back have double purfling. The head, neck, tailpiece, and fingerboard are not original. The head and neck, however, have been restored in old style. The instrument was formerly part of the old Este collection.

Measurements in cm (Boyden): upper bouts: 21.3, center bouts: 15.8, lower bouts: 25.8, depth of sides: 3.8 (Baines[15] gives 3.6 above and 4 below), length of fingerboard: 24.1, string length: 35.3, body length: 42.0 (Baines gives 41), overall length: 65.5 (Baines gives 68).

Pictured in Baines, *Musical Instruments,* no. 15; in Boyden, *Catalogue,* plate 9 a, b, c; and in Witten, "Apollo," p. 27, fig. 20.

8. Lira-viola by an anonymous Italian (Brescian or Venetian) maker of the 16th century. Location: Musikinstrumenten-Museum, Berlin (No. 2578).

Sachs[16] describes the instrument as being closely related to the Linarol instrument of 1580 in Vienna (Schlosser catalogue no. C. 108), which has almost the same measurements. It has the characteristic lira da braccio indented lower end and the stripes of inlay on the back, as on the Vienna instrument. There is double purfling on the table only, which has early forms of F-holes (S-shaped). The head and neck (fingerboard and tailpiece) are not original. The instrument, more recently described in a Berlin catalog,[17] was restored under the instigation of Curt Sachs to an original lira da braccio form.

Measurements in cm. (Otto/Adelmann): upper bouts: 21.4, lower bouts: 26.6, body depth: 3.9 (average), body length: 46.7, overall length: 78.6.

Pictured in Munrow, *Instruments*, p. 136 (as restored lira da braccio); in Otto/Adelmann, *Katalog*, p. 99 (line drawing); in W. Stauder, *Alte Musikinstrumente*, p. 186 (as lira da braccio); and in Sachs, *Sammlung*, plate 15 (as viola).

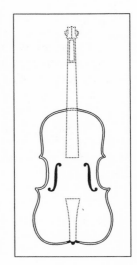

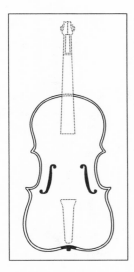

9. Lira-viola by Ventura Linarol, Venice, 1580. Label written in ink: Ventura di Fran<u>eo</u> Linarol in Venetia 1580. Located in the Kunsthistorischen Museum (Schlosser catalog no. C. 108), Vienna.

Schlosser[18] describes the instrument as having a golden yellow varnish. The back has striped inlay in the manner of black-white-black purfling.[19] The instrument has the characteristic lira da braccio indented base at the tailpiece. The head and tailpiece (neck and fingerboard) are not original, and in its present viola form, the instrument has four strings. The table has an early form of F-holes (S-form). This instrument is closely related in size and appearance to the anonymous instrument in the Berlin museum (no. 2578).

Measurements in cm (Schlosser): upper bouts: 22.5, lower bouts: 26.5, depth of sides: 4, body length: 47.5, overall length: 70.

Pictured in Schlosser, *Sammlung*, vol. 3, plate XXIII, no. 108.

10. Lira-viola attributed to Gasparo da Salò,[20] Brescia. Located in the Music Conservatory Museum (Mahillon[21] catalog III, no. 1415), Brussels.

Only the body of the instrument is original. A very large instrument with complex C-holes.

Measurements in cm (Mahillon): lower bouts: 35.5, overall length: 86. More measurements given in Baines:[22] body length: 53.3, depth 5.5. In its present viola form there are four strings.

Pictured in Baines, *Musical Instruments*, no. 12, and in Geiser, *Studien*, instrument illustration II.

Notes

1. Witten, "Apollo," p. 46.
2. Boyden, *Catalog*, p. 14.
3. Baines, *Musical Instruments*, p. 7.
4. Described in Mahillon, *Catalogue*, vol. 3, p. 59. See also Witten, "Apollo," p. 46.
5. Parson, *Organological Study*, p. 74.
6. Disertori, "L'Arciviolatalira," p. 208.
7. Parson and Disertori measurements probably taken from Mahillon.
8. Description in Baines, *Musical Instruments*, p. 7.
9. Description of the instrument and the translation of the Latin is taken from Monical, *Shapes of the Baroque*.
10. Schlosser, *Sammlung*, vol. 3, p. 65. See also Witten, "Apollo," p. 30.
11. For further information on the Heyer collection, see Coover, *Musical Instrument Collections*, p. 336.
12. Kinsky, *Katalog*, p. 415.
13. This date is questioned in Witten, "Apollo," p. 26.
14. Boyden, *Catalogue*, p. 16.
15. Baines, *Musical Instruments*, p. 9.
16. Sachs, *Sammlung*, p. 137. See also Witten, "Apollo," p. 49.
17. Otto/Adelmann, *Katalog*, p. 100.
18. Schlosser, *Sammlung*, p. 68.
19. Witten, "Apollo," p. 48.
20. Witten, "Apollo," p. 26. Witten does not support this attribution.
21. Mahillon, *Catalogue*, p. 44.
22. Baines, *Musical Instruments*, p. 9.

Comparative Sizes of Six Extant Lira da Braccio Instruments

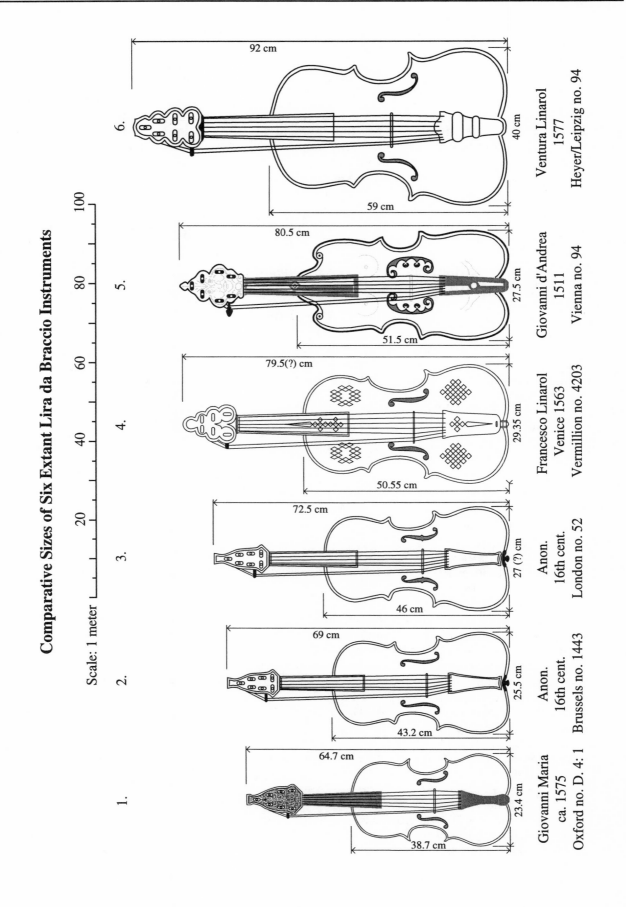

Scale: 1 meter

1.   2.   3.   4.   5.   6.

Ventura Linarol
1577
Heyer/Leipzig no. 94

92 cm
59 cm
40 cm

Giovanni d'Andrea
1511
Vienna no. 94

80.5 cm
51.5 cm
27.5 cm

Francesco Linarol
Venice 1563
Vermillion no. 4203

79.5(?) cm
50.55 cm
29.35 cm

Anon.
16th cent.
London no. 52

72.5 cm
46 cm
27 (?) cm

Anon.
16th cent.
Brussels no. 1443

69 cm
43.2 cm
25.5 cm

Giovanni Maria
ca. 1575
Oxford no. D. 4: 1

64.7 cm
38.7 cm
23.4 cm

Comparative Sizes of Four Lira-violas (Originally Lira da Braccio Instruments?)

Scale: 1 meter

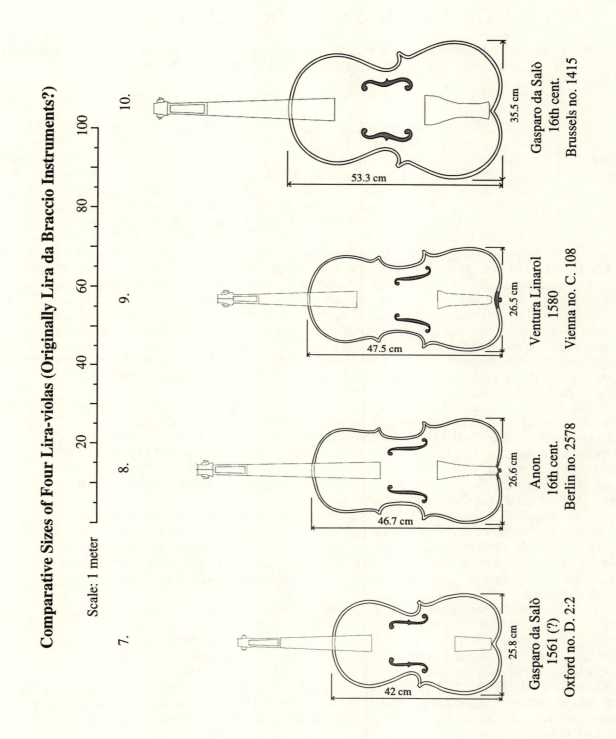

7.

8.

9.

10.

Gasparo da Salò
1561 (?)
Oxford no. D. 2:2

25.8 cm
42 cm

Anon.
16th cent.
Berlin no. 2578

26.6 cm
46.7 cm

Ventura Linarol
1580
Vienna no. C. 108

26.5 cm
47.5 cm

Gasparo da Salò
16th cent.
Brussels no. 1415

35.5 cm
53.3 cm

20   40   60   80   100

4

The Lira da Braccio in Works of Art

(Instruments marked with an asterisk may be found in the Music Instrument Picture Collection, Uta Henning, Bismarckstrasse 32, 71634 Ludwigsburg, Germany)

Instruments with Bodies Having Four Corners (Type A)

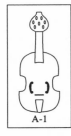

A-1. Woodcuts: from an edition of Ovid's *Metamorphoses.* Illustrations of Apollo playing a large lira. Bagpipes and a pan flute are also shown. Published in Venice in 1497, 1501. Pictured below on p. 121 (detail); in Disertori, "Pratica," pp. 173, 175 (1497 version); in Kinsky, *Katalog,* p. 413; Winternitz, *Leonardo,* p. 35, ex. 4.10; and in Winternitz, *Symbolism,* pp. 158-59 (1501 version). Five strings on fingerboard with two lowest strings closer together, one off. Six pegs seem to be indicated. Curved bridge set below C-holes, which face inward. Body ends not indented. Long arched bow held away from instrument (a = fol. 49v). Short, arched bow on strings at tip near bridge, large frog (b = fol. 143r). Hand position on bow away from end in both examples. The latter example seems to indicate fingers on hair of bow.

A-2. Engraving: by an anonymous "Master of the Sforza Book of Hours," showing an angel playing a lira (or viola) da braccio with another angel playing a lute. Milan (?), ca. 1500. Pictured in Hind, *Engravings,* vol. VII, plate 602; in Witten, "Apollo," p. 29, fig. 22 (detail). An ornate instrument with four scrolled corners, the top body end indentation also showing scrolled construction. C-holes in upper bouts face inward, reflecting the center bouts. Strings, bridge, and pegs not indicated. Fingerboard has frets. Body end is covered by an ornate tailpiece but appears to be indented; top end indented. Medium length, arched bow on strings in middle of bow. Small frog as part of stick. Hand position on bow at end.

A-3. Bronze plaque: *Orpheus and Eurydice,* showing Orpheus holding a lira da braccio. One of a series of four plaques by Moderno dealing with the Orpheus cycle, ca. 1500. National Gallery of Art, Washington. Pictured in Pope-Hennessy, *Renaissance Bronzes,* no. 173, ill. 198. Another one in the series entitled *Orpheus in Hades* is pictured in MGG, vol. 8, p. 944; in Winternitz, *Leonardo,* p. 26, ex. 4.2; and in Winternitz, *Symbolism,* plate 30-b. No details are visible. C-holes face inward. Body ends not indented. No bow shown.

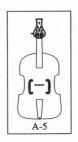

A-4. Woodcut: Cristoforo Scultore, *Capitoli,* shows a youth holding a lira (or viola) da braccio, another with a shawm. Florence, ca. 1505. Pictured in Sander, *Le Livre,* no. 2245; in Witten, "Apollo," p. 31, fig. 24 (detail). Strings and pegs unclear. Bridge placed below C-holes, which face inward. Rare example of straight center bouts. Body ends not indented. Short, straight bow held away from instrument. Large frog. Hand position on bow away from end.

A-5. Painting: *Coronation of the Virgin,* with detail showing a very large lira da braccio played by a young woman (angel). Giovanni Bellini, 1505, San Zaccaria, Venice. Pictured in Disertori, "Pratica," p. 160 (detail); in Heydenreich, *Universum der Kunst,* p. 281; in *La pittura,* p. 152; in Winternitz, *Leonardo,* p. 29, ex. 4.4 (detail); in Winternitz, *Symbol,* plate 33-a (detail); and in *Early Music,* vol. 21, no. 4 (November 1993), p. 583 (detail). Five equidistant strings on fingerboard, two off, spaced somewhat farther apart. Bridge is slightly curved and set high between large C-holes, which face inward. Seven pegs. Body ends not indented. Light, long, arched bow placed on strings at middle, far from bridge. No visible frog. Hand position on bow at end.

A-6. Woodcut: in an edition of Ovid, *Epistolae Heroides,* showing a woman with a lira (or viola) da braccio. Venice, 10.VIII.1510. Pictured in Essling, *Les Livres,* no. 1136; in Witten, "Apollo," p. 29, fig. 23 (detail). Only two strings on fingerboard shown, but four pegs. Indistinct

C-holes placed low, facing inward. No bridge indicated. Body ends not indented. Medium length, high arched bow off strings. Large frog. Hand position on bow away from end.

A-7. Painting: *Apollo,* with lira da braccio. Spagna Giovanni di Pietro (Lospangna), 1503-13. Pinacoteca Capitolina, Rome. Pictured in Geiser, *Studien*, no. 71. Number of strings unclear. C-holes face inward. Bottom end unclear, top not indented. Light, medium length, arched bow, off strings. Medium-size frog. Hand position on bow away from end.

A-8. Intarsia: showing a lira da braccio with bow and lute. Fra Vincenzo da Verona, ca. 1515. Louvre Museum, Paris. Pictured in Geiser, *Studien*, no. 72. Number of strings unclear. Bridge slightly curved, placed low between S-shaped holes. Seven pegs. Body ends not indented. Bow length unclear, straight stick with medium size frog, placed behind instrument.

A-9. Engraving: Orpheus shown playing a lira (or viola) da braccio. Marcantonio Raimondi, Rome (?), ca. 1515. Pictured in Essling, *Les Livres*, no. 2136; in Witten, "Apollo," p. 32, fig. 27 (detail). Six strings all on a fingerboard, which has frets. Sixth string appears to be farther apart from others. Six pegs. Bridge not shown. Large C-holes face inward. Bottom end of body appears to be slightly indented. High arched, short bow on strings at tip. No frog. Hand position on bow at end.

A-10. Woodcut: In edition of *Lauretum,* a collection of verses dedicated to Lorenzo de Medici, showing a poet-musician with lira (or viola) da braccio. Florence, 1516. Biblioteca Nazionale, Florence. Pictured in Abbiati, *Storia,* p. 367. Two strings shown but three pegs. Bridge set below C-holes, which face inward. Body ends not indented. Arched bow of medium length not on strings. Medium-size frog. Hand position on bow away from end with fingers appearing to be on hair.

A-11. Engraving: *Apollo and the Graces,* Apollo shown playing a large lira da braccio, Graces with recorders. Engraving by Marcantonio Raimondi (ca. 1480-ca. 1530) based on painting by Francesco Francia (ca. 1480-1517). State Museum, Berlin, Kupferstich-kabinett. Pictured in *Das klingende Jahr*, 1972 issue (Leipzig, Breitkopf & Härtel). Seven strings, all on fingerboard, the second and third strings placed close together on a bridge set just below large C-holes curved slightly outward. Seven pegs. Bottom end of body indented. High arched, short bow on strings at middle, far from bridge. Large frog. Hand position on bow at end.*

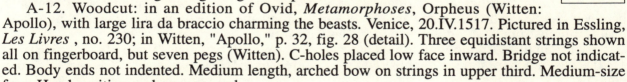

A-12. Woodcut: in an edition of Ovid, *Metamorphoses*, Orpheus (Witten: Apollo), with large lira da braccio charming the beasts. Venice, 20.IV.1517. Pictured in Essling, *Les Livres* , no. 230; in Witten, "Apollo," p. 32, fig. 28 (detail). Three equidistant strings shown all on fingerboard, but seven pegs (Witten). C-holes placed low face inward. Bridge not indicated. Body ends not indented. Medium length, arched bow on strings in upper third. Medium-size frog. Hand position on bow near end.

A-13. Engraving: *Apollo and Pan,* with Apollo playing a lira (or viola) da braccio and Pan holding panpipes. Benedetto Montagna, not after 1520 (Witten). Pictured in Hind, *Engravings*, vol. VII, plate 763; in Witten, "Apollo," p. 34, fig. 30 (detail). Five strings all on fingerboard. No pegs shown. Bridge placed low or just below C-holes, which face inward. Body ends not indented. Medium length, arched bow on strings at middle, far from bridge. Frog not visible. Hand position on bow at end.

A-14. Engraving: *Apollo and Marsyas,* with Apollo holding a lira (or viola) da braccio and Marsyas playing bagpipes. Benedetto Montagna, not after 1520 (Witten). Pictured in Hind, *Engravings*, vol. VII, plate 763; in Witten, "Apollo," p. 35, fig. 31 (detail). Three equidistant strings shown, all on fingerboard. Bridge placed near tailpiece far below ornate C-holes, which face outward. Additional small round holes are placed on lower bouts. Pegs not indicated. Bottom end of body appears to be indented, top end not. Unusual shape with an additional set of corners on lower bouts. Bow, held away from instrument, appears to be fairly long although tip does not show. Medium-size frog. Hand position on bow away from end.

A-15. Woodcut: *Istoria et favola di Orfeo.* Orpheus shown playing a lira or viola da braccio. Siena, ca. 1520 (Witten). Pictured above on p. 6; in Disertori, "Pratica," p. 172 (with same woodcut used as title page with date 1605); in Sander, *Le Livre*, no. 5220; in Witten, "Apollo," p.

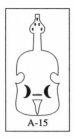

A-15

35, fig. 32 (detail). Four equidistant strings on fingerboard. Five pegs implied but only four visible, one peg being covered by an extended finger. Bridge set low between C-holes, which face outward. Bottom end of body appears to be slightly indented. Short, arched bow held away from instrument. No frog visible. Hand position away from end.

A-16. Painting: *The Concert*. Lira or viola da braccio played by male with singer, tranverse flute, and bass gamba or violone. Bonifazio di Pitati, ca. 1520. Location? Pictured in Geiser, *Studien*, no. 73 (detail). Only back side of instrument shown. Top end of body not indented, bottom end not visible. Bow presumably on strings at middle, only top end visible.

A-17. Painting: *Madonna di Trino*, showing a lira da braccio and a cherub holding a bow. Ottaviano Cane, 1535. Torino, Galleria Sabauda. Pictured in *La pittura*, p. 48, no. 47. Four equidistant strings on fingerboard, one off. Pegbox not fully visible but two upright pegs show. Curved bridge placed low between S-shaped holes, which are placed high and are horizontally reversed. Indentation only at top end of the body. Medium length, arched bow held away from instrument. Medium-size frog. Hand position on bow at end.

A-18. Charcoal drawing: *Apollo and Marsia*. Apollo with a lira da braccio and Marsia holding what appear to be panpipes. Copy by Anton Maria Zanetti, 1724, of a Parmigianino painting (1505-1540). Pictured in Disertori, "Pratica," no. 45, p. 170. Strings not shown. Other details not clear. Sound holes unclear. Bottom end of body not visible, top end not indented. Medium-length bow, arched near tip, held away from instrument. Frog unclear. Hand position on bow at end.

A-19. Drawing: Three women playing lira da braccio, violone, and harp. Gaudenzio Ferrari, ca. 1545. British Museum, London. Pictured in Geiser, *Studien*, no. 74. Number of strings unclear. Five pegs plus possible indication of one string off the fingerboard, with peg or pin on side of pegbox. Bridge unclear. Large S-shaped holes. Body ends not indented. Medium length, high arched bow on strings at middle. Frog not visible. Hand position on bow away from end with fingers appearing to touch hair.

A-20. Woodcut: in edition of Angelo Poliziano, *Favola d'Orfeo*, shows Orfeo with a lira (or viola) da braccio charming the animals. Florence, ca. 1550, but the woodblock ca. 1500-20 (Witten). Pictured in Sander, *Le Livre*, no. 6318; in Witten, "Apollo," p. 33, fig. 29 (detail). Three equidistant strings all on fingerboard, but five pegs are shown. Bridge placed centrally between C-holes, which face inward. Body ends not indented. Medium length, arched bow held away from instrument. Medium-size frog. Hand position on bow away from end.

A-21. Painting: Apollo with lira da braccio, Marsyas with bagpipes. Titian (1477?-1576), ca. 1570. Museum Kromeriz, Czechoslovakia. Pictured in *UMENI*, issue 9, 1961, p. 327. Four equidistant strings indicated, possibly five between bridge and tailpiece. Pin on side of pegbox would imply off-the-fingerboard string(s). Seven pegs. Curved bridge placed well below F-holes uniquely formed in four parts (ʃ ʅ). Body ends not indented. Medium length, arched bow, held away from strings. Frog unclear. Hand position on bow away from end.

A-22. Pen and ink drawing: Costume study for a procession in Vienna with musician holding a lira da braccio and bow in right hand. Giuseppe Arcimboldo (1527-1593), 1571. Uffizi, (Collection of Engravings), Florence. Pictured in *Prag um 1600. Kunst und Kultur am Hofe Kaiser Rudolfs II*, vol. I, Freren, 1988, no. 189. Three equidistant strings indicated, but number of pegs unclear. Bridge placed low between C-holes, which face inward. Indentation at both ends of body indicated. Short, low arched bow, held with instrument. Small frog.*

A-23. Woodcut: lira da braccio in foreground of scene with praying David in *Breviarium Congregationis Casinensis*, Venice, 1575. Pictured in Essling, *Les Livres*, no. 1097; and in Witten, "Apollo," p. 45, fig. 44 (detail). Four equidistant strings on fingerboard, two off. A curved bridge is set low between S-shaped holes. Number of pegs unclear. Lower end of body indented. Short, arched bow shown behind instrument. Medium-size frog.

A-24. Painting: *Concert of Nymphs*, with lira da braccio and bow lying in foreground. A bass viol and a positive organ are also shown. Tintoretto, ca. 1582-84, Dresden, Gemäldegalerie. Pictured in Bosseur, *Musique*, p. 59; in *Early Music*, vol. XVIII, No. 2 (May, 1989), p. 161; in

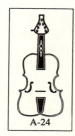

A-24

Kinsky, *Katalog*, p. 395; in Kinsky, *Geschichte*, p. 113, ill. 2; in Moreck, *Die Musik*, p. 35; and in Sauerlandt, *Die Musik,* p. 77. Five strings on fingerboard, grouped from top down: 2+2+1, two or three (?) strings off. Bridge slightly curved, set low between F-shaped holes. Seven pegs. Body indentation at bottom end. Short, low arched bow with medium-sized frog next to instrument.

A-25. Engraving: Representation of Jupiter holding a lira da braccio. From Vincenzo Cartari, *Le Imagini dei Dei degli Antichi*, 1580. Pictured in MGG, vol. 8, p. 946; also in Winternitz, *Symbolism*, p. 93. Eight equidistant strings on fingerboard, one off, total of nine strings, as described in text. A curved bridge is placed very low. Eight pegs plus one on side. C-holes face outward (E-form). Body ends not indented. No bow.

A-26. Drawing: male figure with lira da braccio. Luca da Cambiaso (1527-85). Uffizi Museum, Florence. Pictured in Winternitz, *Symbolism*, plate 3-b. Strings not shown. Pegs unclear (five?). C-holes face outward. Top end of body indented, bottom end unclear. Long, high arched bow held away from instrument. Small-size frog. Hand position on bow at end.

A-27. Watercolor study: Orpheus with lira (viola) da braccio charming the animals. Johann Melchior (Hans Jr.) Bocksberger (before 1540-1589). Munich, Staatl. Graph. Sammlung: Inv.-no. 1951/80. Pictured in Musica-Kalender, 1990 issue: *Apollo-David-Orpheus* (Kassel: Bärenreiter-Verlag). Number of strings (four?) and pegs unclear. Bridge (curved?) placed low between very large S-shaped holes. Ends of body not indented. Short, high arched bow on strings at middle, near bridge. No frog. Hand position on bow at end.

A-28. Painting: *King David,* with lira da braccio. Bartolommeo Passerotti (1529-1592). Galleria Spada, Rome. Pictured in MGG, vol. 8, plate 37-1; and in Winternitz, *Symbolism*, plate 32-a. Five equidistant strings on fingerboard, two off. A curved bridge is set low between F-holes. Seven pegs. Ends of body not indented but both upper and lower bouts have scalloped indentations. Short, arched bow held away from instrument. Large frog. Hand position on bow at end.

A-28

A-29. Engraving: Apollo playing a lira da braccio enchanting a diversified collection of animals. Illustration on the back side of the title page in Giovanni Luca Conforto, *Breue et Facile Maniera D'Essercitarsi a Far Passaggi,* (Rome 1593 [or 1603?]. Published in facsimile edition with German translation by Johannes Wolf (Berlin: Verlag Martin Breslauer, 1922). Pictured also in Geiser, *Studien,* no. XXIII (detail). Five equidistant strings on fingerboard, two (?) off. Number of pegs (seven?) unclear. Bridge set centrally between C-holes, which face outward. Ends of body not indented. Short, low arched bow held off strings. Frog not visible. Hand position on bow at end.

A-30. Engraving: A "lirone da braccio" (large lira da braccio) player with instrument held across the chest supported by the right upper arm. Giambattista Bracelli, 1599. Pictured in Kinsky, *Katalog,* p. 413. Four equidistant strings shown, but six pegs. No bridge shown. S-shaped holes. Bottom end of body not visible, top end not indented. Short, arched bow on strings at middle. Medium-size frog. Hand position on bow away from end.

A-31. Plaque: for the musical scholar Ercole Bottrigari, early 17th century. Pictured in MGG, vol. 8, p. 950; and in Winternitz, *Symbolism*, plate 30-a. Four equidistant strings on fingerboard, two off. Six (?) pegs. S-shaped holes. No bridge indicated. Ends of body not indented. Medium-length bow with high arch near tip shown behind instrument.

A-32. Painting: *Allegory of Hearing*, lira da braccio shown with various other instruments. Jan Bruegel the Elder, 1617. Prado, Madrid. Pictured in Bosseur, *Musique*, p. 62; in Geiser, *Studien*, no. 75 (detail); in Kinsky, *Geschichte*, p. 151; in New Grove Dictionary, vol. 11, p. 19 (detail); and in Winternitz, *Symbol*, plate 37-a (detail). Four equidistant strings on fingerboard, two strings off close together, but seven pegs shown. Flat bridge set low between F-holes. Ends of body not indented. Very short bow with low arched, almost straight stick, placed beside instrument. Medium-size frog.

A-33. Illustration in *Syntagma Musicum*, vol. 3, *De Organographia*, plate XX. Lira da braccio shown with other bowed string instruments. Michael Praetorius, 1619. Pictured in

Bessaraboff, *Instruments,* p. 361; in Geiser, *Studien,* no. 76; and in W. Stauder, *Alte Musik-instrumente,* p. 186. Five strings on fingerboard, two lowest close together. Two strings off, close together. Fingerboard has frets. Seven pegs. Bridge placed centrally between F-holes. Body ends not indented. Short, straight bow with medium-size frog shown beside instrument.

A-34. Painting: *Homer,* playing a lira da braccio held transversely across chest. Jusepe Ribera (1588-1652). Pictured in Kinsky, *Katalog,* p. 399 (19th-century copper engraving by Bedetti after a drawing by L. Metalli of the painting). Four equidistant strings on fingerboard, with more space between the two strings off the fingerboard. A flat bridge is placed slightly diagonally closer to tailpiece on left side and somewhat lower than central between F-holes. Pegs unclear. Indented lower end of body. Medium length, low arched bow on strings at middle, far from bridge. Frog not visible. Hand position on bow away from end.

A-35. Woodcut: detail showing a lira da braccio with bow and several other instruments. Joachim de Flore, *Profetie* (Padua, 1625). Last appearance of a lira da braccio in a Veneto graphic (Witten). Pictured in Witten, "Apollo," p. 49, fig. 47 (detail). Six strings on fingerboard with lowest three closer together, two strings off placed close together. A curved bridge is set low between S-shaped holes. Seven pegs plus one peg or pin on the side. Indented lower end of body. Short, low arched bow lying diagonally across strings. Medium-size frog.

A-36. Sketches: "Orpheus and Eurydice," with three lira da braccio instruments. Odoardo Fialetti (1577-1638). Barry Brook Collection, New York. Number of strings and pegs unclear. One sketch shows bridge placement halfway between S-shaped holes and tailpiece. Ends of bodies not indented. Short, high arched bows, one shown on strings at middle very far from bridge. Frog unclear. Hand position on bow at end.*

A-37. Painting: *Contest between Apollo and Marsyas,* shows Apollo playing a large lira da braccio and Marsyas holding panpipes. Jacopo Palma, called Palma il Giovane (1544-1628). Herzog Anton Ulrich-Museum, Braunschweig. Pictured in Musica-Kalender, 1990 issue: *Apollo-David-Orpheus* (Kassel: Bärenreiter-Verlag). Five equidistant strings on fingerboard, two off somewhat farther apart. Curved bridge set low between F-holes. Pegs and pegbox not visible. Body ends not indented. Short, arched bow on top string near frog rather far from bridge. Medium-sized frog. Hand position on bow away from end with first and second fingers on hair.

Instruments with Bodies Having Only Two Corners (Type B)

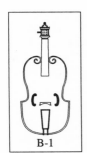

B-1. Woodcut: from *Carmina*, G. A. Augurello. Illustration of a lira da braccio with bow (original print reversed). Published in Verona, 5.VII.1491, (p. 667). Pictured in Sander, *Le Livre*, no. 667; in Witten, "Apollo," p. 20, fig. 10. Five strings on fingerboard, two lowest closer together, two off close together. Seven pegs. Flat bridge set low between C-holes, which face inward. Bottom end of body not indented but top end indented with scroll designs on body. Bow, medium length, straight stick with small frog, placed next to instrument.

B-2. Woodcut: *Officia*, an illustrated prayer book showing psalmist King David playing a lira da braccio. Venice, 1494. Pictured in Essling, *Les Livres,* 457; and in Witten, "Apollo," p. 21, fig. 11 (detail). Four equidistant strings on fingerboard, one off. Five pegs. Bridge set below C-holes, which face inward. Ends of body not indented. Short, arched bow on strings near tip, far from bridge. No frog. Hand position on bow away from end.

B-3. Intarsia: a lira da braccio with other instruments. Camerini d'Isabella in the Ducal Palace, Mantua, late 15th century. Pictured in *Early Music,* vol. 3, no. 4 (October 1975), p. 342; and in *Early Music,* vol. 9, no. 4 (October 1981), p. 459, fig. 5. Strings unclear but at least one shown on fingerboard and two off. Four pegs shown, others missing. Slightly curved bridge placed a bit lower than center between C-holes, which face inward. Body ends not indented. No bow.

B-4. Painting: *Asolani.* Court of Catarina Cornaro with two lute players and a lira da braccio player. A view of Asolo is in the background. School of Giorgione, ca. 1500. Attingham Park, Shrewsbury, Shropshire. Pictured in Bertelli, *Italian Renaissance Courts*, p. 11. Strings and pegs unclear. Bridge placed centrally between inward-facing C-holes. Bottom end of body unclear, top end not indented. Short, medium arched bow on strings at middle, far from bridge. Frog unclear. Hand position on bow away from end with fingers appearing to be on hair.

B-5. Painting: *Madonna and Child with Saints.* Lira da braccio player with two lute players, one tuning his instrument. Bartolommeo Montagna, 1505. Pinacoteca di Brera, Milan. Pictured in Capri, *Storia,* p. 263; in Disertori, "Pratica," 45, p. 158 (detail); in Disertori, *Le Frottole (1964),* plate XV; in Geiser, *Studien,* no. 63 (detail); in Kinsky, *Katalog,* p. 391; and in Kinsky, *Geschichte,* p. 111, ill. 3. Five strings on fingerboard with more space between fourth and fifth, plus two strings off placed close together. A curved bridge is set low between C-holes, which face inward. Seven pegs. Bottom end of body unclear, top end not indented. Low arched, long bow on strings near tip at normal distance from bridge. Small frog. Hand position on bow away from end.

B-6. Engraving: *Orpheus,* playing a lira da braccio (print reversed). Benedetto Montagna, ca. 1505. Graphische Sammlung der Albertina, Vienna. Pictured in Hind, *Engravings,* vol. VII, plate 745; in Abbiati, *Storia,* p. 487; in Geiser, *Studien,* no. 62; in Winternitz, *Leonardo,* p. 31, ex. 4.5; and in Witten, "Apollo," p. 25, fig. 16 (detail). Only four equidistant strings shown on fingerboard, but tailpiece indicates seven strings, two off close together. Seven pegs shown. Bridge set near tailpiece below C-holes, which face inward. Ends of body not indented. Low arched, long bow on strings at upper middle, very close to bridge. Small frog. Hand position on bow away from end.

B-7. Painting: *Coronation of the Virgin,* showing one angel playing a lira da braccio, another a rebec. Raphael Santi, 1505. Pinacoteca Vaticana, Rome. Pictured in *Arte Cristiana,* nos. 737-38, p. 172, no. 3; in Francia, *Pinacoteca,* no. 223; and in Sauerlandt, *Die Musik,* p. 49. Appear to be five strings on fingerboard, two off. Five upright pegs plus one on side. Bridge possibly curved, set low between large C-holes. Bottom end of body unclear but appears not to be indented. Upper end not indented. High arched, long bow on strings at middle, appearing to be rather far from bridge. Frog unclear. Hand position on bow at end.

B-8. Painting: *Ascension of Maria.* Angel playing a lira da braccio. Mariotto Albertinelli, ca. 1506. Berlin (?). Pictured in Geiser, *Studien,* no. 64 (detail). Number of strings unclear, but at least one string off the fingerboard. Number of pegs unclear. Bridge (unclear) placed centrally between large C-holes, which face inward. Ends of body not indented. Large frog. Arched, long bow on strings at middle. Hand position on bow away from end.

B-9. Painting: *Madonna and Child with Saints* showing angel with lira da braccio. Cima Giovanni Battista da Conegliano, ca. 1510. Galleria Nazionale, Parma. Pictured in Geiser, *Studien,* no. 66 (detail). Five strings on fingerboard, with two off. Total of seven equidistant strings on a slightly curved bridge set centrally between C-holes, which face inward. Seven pegs. Ends of body not indented. Short, arched bow held away from instrument. Medium-size frog. Hand position on bow away from end. See Frontispiece.

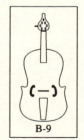
B-9

B-10. Painting: *Group of Musicians.* A detail showing player tuning a lira da braccio. Jacopo Palma il vecchio, ca. 1510. Private collection. Pictured in Geiser, *Studien,* no. 2 (detail). Rare example of instrument with two corners on upper bouts. Four equidistant strings on fingerboard, one off. Pegs and bridge not clear. S-shaped holes. Body ends not indented. No bow.

B-11. Painting: *Annunciation.* Angel with lira da braccio. Mariotto Albertinelli, 1510. Uffizi, Florence. Pictured in Geiser, *Studien,* no. 24 (detail). Number of strings unclear, but at least four show. Five pegs. Bridge centrally located between C-holes which face inward. Ends of body not indented. Arched short bow on or near strings at bottom end, far from bridge. Frog unclear. Hand position on bow away from end.

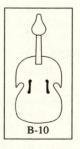
B-10

B-12. Painting: *Presentation in the Temple*. Angels with lira da braccio, lute, and crumhorn. Vittore Carpaccio, ca. 1510. Accademia, Venice. Drawing of the lira da braccio in Baines, *Musical Instruments,* p. 7. Pictured in Disertori, "Pratica," p. 162; in Geiser, *Studien,* no. 65; in Kinsky, *Geschicht ,* p. 143, ill. 2; in Winternitz, *Leonardo,* p. 31, ex. 4.6; and in Winternitz, *Symbolism,* plate 33-b. This is probably the instrument referred to by Vasari (see above, pp. 3, 7). Five strings on fingerboard with more space between third, fourth, and fifth, plus two strings off, closer together. A slightly curved bridge is centrally located between C-holes, which face inward. Seven pegs. Ends of body not indented. Short, arched bow held away from instrument. Frog unclear. Hand position on bow away from end

B-13. Drawing: study for *Parnassus*. Raphael Santi, 1508-11. Palais des Beaux-Arts, Lille. Pictured in Geiser, *Studien,* no. 67; and in Winternitz, *Symbolism,* plate 84-b. Four equidistant strings on fingerboard, plus two strings off, close together. A curved bridge is set low between C-holes, which face inward. Appear to be six upright pegs, plus one peg (or pin) on the side. Ends of body not indented. Long, arched bow on strings at middle, placed at normal playing distance from bridge. Frog unclear. Hand position on bow at end.

B-14. Fresco: *Parnassus*. Apollo playing a lira da braccio. Raphael Santi, ca. 1511. Stanza della Segnatura, Vatican, Rome. Pictured in Bosseur, *Musique,* pp. 48-49; in Disertori, *Le Frottole* (1954), p. LXXVII; in Heydenreich, *Universum der Kunst,* p. 217, no. 215; in Kinsky, *Geschichte,* p. 143, ill. 3 (detail); in Munrow, *Musikinstrumente,* p. 137; and in Winternitz, *Symbolism,* plate 78 and plate 84-a (detail). From top down: 2+2+3 strings on fingerboard, two off, total of nine strings symbolizing the nine Muses. Eight pegs upright, one lateral peg on the side. Slightly curved bridge set low between C-holes, which face inward. Top end of body not indented. Bottom end unclear but not indented in drawing (see B-13). Long, arched bow on strings in upper part of bow at normal distance from bridge. Small frog. Hand position on bow at end.

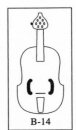

B-14

B-15. Woodcut: humanist with lira da braccio, from *De Syllabarum quantitate*. Quitianus Stoa, 1511. Pictured in *Early Music,* vol. 10, no. 4 (October 1982), p. 427, fig. 2; in MGG, vol. 8, p. 947; in Winternitz, *Leonardo,* p. 37, ex. 4.13; and in Winternitz, *Symbolism,* p. 95. Three equidistant strings on fingerboard, plus one off (on reversed side). A curved bridge is placed low between C-holes, which face inward. Number of pegs unclear. Bottom end of body indented, top end not. Arched, short bow separate from instrument. Medium-size frog.

B-16. Painting: *The Mystic Marraige of St. Catherine,* showing two angels, one playing a lira da braccio, the other a lute. Fra Bartolommeo, 1512. Accademia, Florence. Pictured in *Encyclopedia of World Art,* Vol. XII, pl. 64. Five equidistant strings on fingerboard, two off. Bridge is placed low between large C-holes, which face inward. Bridge appears to be slightly curved. Seven pegs. Ends of body not indented. Arched long bow on strings in upper part of bow, far from bridge. Medium-size frog. Hand position on bow away from end.

B-17. Intarsia: choir stall showing a lira da braccio with two different sized tambourines. Santa Maria in Organo, Verona. Pictured in MGG, vol. 8, plate 38-1; in Winternitz, *Leonardo,* p. 29, ex. 4.3; and in Winternitz, *Symbolism,* plate 34-a. Five equidistant strings on fingerboard, plus two strings off, close together, but spaced farther away from other five. A curved bridge is set high between large C-holes, which face inward. Seven pegs. Bottom end of body is slightly indented, top end not indented. Straight, long bow separate from instrument. Large frog.

B-18. Woodcut: in an *Officium,* showing a lira (or viola) da braccio in the foreground with a kneeling David in prayer. Venice, 1.IX.1512. Pictured in Essling, *Les Livres,* no. 479; in Witten, "Apollo," p. 22, fig. 12 (detail). Three equidistant strings, all on fingerboard. Pegs partly obscured. Bridge placed centrally between C-holes, which face inward and are placed low. Bottom end of body not indented, but top end indented with scroll design. Short, straight bow shown separate from instrument. Medium-size frog.

B-19. Woodcut: In an edition of Pasquillus, *Versi posti . . . ,* Apollo (?) with drawing of a large lira with flute. Rome, 1513. Pictured in Sander, *Le Livre,* no. 5445; in Witten, "Apollo," p. 22, fig. 13 (detail). Six equidistant strings all on fingerboard with six pegs. Flat bridge placed near tailpiece below C-holes, which face inward. Top end of body indented but not bottom end. High arched bow partly shown behind instrument.

B-20. Woodcut: Title page of Antonio Carmigiano, *Le cose vulgare,* Apollo and the Muses, showing Apollo playing a lira da braccio and others playing cymbals, long trumpet, a cornetto-type instrument, a plucked instrument, and a recorder. Venice, 23.XII.1516. Pictured in Essling, *Les Livres,* no. 1916. Three equidistant strings on fingerboard but seven pegs shown. Bridge set below C-holes placed low, which face inward. Ends of body not indented. Arched, medium-length bow on strings in upper part of bow, far from bridge. Medium-size frog. Hand position on bow away from end, with some fingers appearing to be on hair.

B-21. Painting/drawing: *Ascension of Maria,* with detail showing angel playing a lira da braccio. Fra Bartolomeo (1472-1517), dated 1516. Museo Nazionale, Naples. Pictured in Geiser, *Studien,* no. 23 (detail). The same angel and other angels with lutes and horns are pictured in "La Pala della Signoria di Fra Bartolommeo," in *Critica D'Arte*, Anno LIII, quinta serie n. 17, guign/agosto, 1988, pp. 22-27. This "lira" is possibly the one referred to by Vasari (see above, p. 7). Number of strings and pegs not shown. Bridge placed near tailpiece (in drawing) below very large C-holes placed high, which face inward. Top end of body not indented, lower end unclear. Medium length, arched bow on strings in upper half, close to bridge. Medium-size frog. Hand position on bow away from end.

B-22. Painting: *Madonna and child with angels,* showing one angel with lira da braccio. Vittore Carpaccio, dated 1518. S. Francesco, Pirano. Pictured in Geiser, *Studien,* no. 68 (detail). Number of strings unclear. Slighly curved bridge has five feet on instrument, set low between C-holes, which face inward. Seven pegs. Bottom end of body unclear, top end not indented. Long bow on strings near tip at normal distance from bridge. Frog unclear. Hand position on bow away from end.

B-23. Painting: *The Virgin and Saints,* with detail showing two angels, one playing a lira da braccio, the other playing a lute. Giambattista Cima da Conegliano (ca. 1459-1517/18). Galleria dell'Accademia, Venice. Pictured in Remnant, *Musical Instruments*, p. 52. Four strings on the fingerboard with two lowest somewhat closer together. Unique example of three strings appearing to be off the fingerboard. A curved bridge is placed centrally between C-holes, which face inward. Top end of body not indented, bottom end unclear. Long, low arched bow on strings in upper third at normal playing distance from bridge. Medium-size frog. Hand position on bow away from end.

B-24. Woodcut: In edition of Pietro Aron, *Toscanello in Musica,* drawing of a lira (or viola) da braccio placed on table with lute and recorder. Venice 5.VII.1519. Copy in British Museum, London: C.31.m.10. Pictured in Abbiati, *Storia,* p. 385 (Frontispiece to 2nd ed., 1529); in Essling, *Les Livres*, no. 2037; and in Witten, "Apollo," p. 23, fig. 14 (detail). Five strings with top string farther from others and lower two closer together. (Only four strings show on the neck). Five pegs. Highly curved bridge placed above low set C-holes, which face inward. Ends of body are not indented. No bow.

B-25. Woodcut: In edition of Folengo, *Macaronea.* A youth is shown playing a large lira (or viola) da braccio. Venice 10. I. 1520. Pictured in Witten, "Apollo," p. 24, fig. 15. Four equidistant strings, all on the fingerboard, but six pegs shown. Bridge unclear. C-holes set low face inward. Body ends not indented. Medium length, arched bow on strings in upper part. Large frog. Hand position on bow away from end with first two fingers on hair, last two behind hair.

B-26. Woodcut: In edition of Luigi Pulci, *Strambotti . . . ,* Orpheus playing a lira (or viola) da braccio charming the animals. Venice, ca. 1525. Pictured in Essling, *Les Livres,* no. 2059; and in Witten, "Apollo," p. 24, fig. 17 (detail). Six strings, all on fingerboard, grouped from top down 3+2+1, but seven pegs. Bridge unclear. C-holes placed high facing outward. Ends of body not indented. Heavy, long, arched bow on strings in upper third. No frog. Hand position on bow away from end, with three fingers on hair and little finger behind hair.

B-27. Woodcut: In edition of Luigi Pulci, *Strambotti . . . ,* Orpheus playing a lira (or viola) da braccio charming the animals. Venice, ca. 1525. Pictured in Essling, *Les Livres,* no. 2537/8; and in Witten, "Apollo," p. 25, fig. 18 (detail). Four equidistant strings, all on fingerboard, which has frets. Five pegs. Highly curved bridge is placed below C-holes, which face inward. Ends of body not indented. Long, arched bow on strings at tip, far from bridge. Medium-size frog as part of stick. Hand position on bow at end.

B-28. Painting: *Sacra conversazione*. A lira da braccio player (angel) performs as soloist before an enthroned Madonna. Palma Vecchio (ca. 1480-1528). San Zaccaria, Venice. Pictured in MGG, vol. 8, plate 43; in Winternitz, *Leonardo*, p. 33, ex. 4.8; and in Winternitz, *Symbolism*, plate 36. Back and side of instrument shown. Body ends not indented. Only top end of bow is visible.

B-29. Painting: *Adoration of the Shepherds*. Angel playing a lira da braccio. Gaudenzio Ferrari, 1532. S. Cristoforo, Vercelli. Pictured in Geiser, *Studien,* no. 70 (detail). Number of strings unclear. Bridge set below reversed S-shaped sound holes. Extension on left side of bridge would indicate string(s) off the fingerboard. Pegs are not all visible. Bottom end of body indented, top end slightly indented. Short, arched bow placed on strings near frog, very far from bridge. Small frog. Hand position on bow away from end.

B-30. Painting: *Allegoria della corte di Isabella d'Este,* with lira da braccio player shown in background (Orpheus?). Lorenzo Costa (1460-1535). Louvre, Paris. Pictured in Bertelli, *Italian Renaissance Courts*, p. 17; in *Early Music,* vol. 4, no. 1 (January, 1976), p. 43; in Disertori, *Le Frottole* (1964), plate II; and in Winternitz, *Leonardo*, p. 71, ex. 5.36 (wrong description, refer to 5.33) and 5.37. Four strings on fretted fingerboard with fourth string somewhat farther apart, one string off. Pegs not visible. Very wide, flat bridge placed below F-shaped holes. Ends of body not indented. Bow appears to be short, arched, on strings in lower part, some distance from bridge. Frog and hand position on bow unclear.

B-31. Painting: *Contest between Apollo and Marsyas*. Apollo plays a lira da braccio, Marsyas holds a bagpipe. Michelangelo Anselmi, ca. 1540. National Gallery, Washington. Pictured in Bosseur, *Musique*, p. 53; in Geiser, *Studien*, no. 69 (detail); in Heydenreich, *Universum der Kunst*, p. 356, no. 360; in Winternitz, *Symbolism,* plates 69-a (detail) and 70-a. Strings and pegs unclear but at least one string shown off the fingerboard. Curved bridge set below C-holes, which face inward. Ends of body not indented. Short, arched, light bow on strings at tip, far from bridge. Frog unclear. Hand position on bow at end.

B-32. Painting: *Apollo,* with lira da braccio. Dosso Dossi (?-1542). Galleria Borghese, Rome. Pictured in Disertori, "Pratica," 45, p. 166 (detail); in Einstein, *The Italian Madrigal*, vol.1, opposite p. 175; and in Kinsky, *Geschichte*, p. 143, ill. 4. Five strings on fingerboard, plus two off. Bridge (possibly curved) is set low between C-holes, which face inward. Seven pegs. Ends of body not indented. Medium length, arched bow held away from instrument. Medium-size frog. Hand position on bow at end.

B-33. Woodcut: in an *Officium*, drawing of a lira da braccio with David (print reversed). Venice, 1544. Pictured in Essling, *Les Livres,* no. 503; and in Witten, "Apollo," p. 27, fig. 19 (detail). Appear to be four strings on fingerboard with one off. Number of pegs unclear. Curved bridge is placed centrally between C-holes, which face inward. Ends of body not indented. Medium arched, short bow separate from instrument. Large frog.

B-34. Painting: *Coronation of the Virgin,* with detail of angel playing a lira da braccio. Other instruments also shown (drum, long trumpets). Ridolfo del Ghirlandaio (1483-1561). Musée du Petit Palais, Avignon. Only the highly ornamented back side of the instrument is visible. Ends of body not indented. Bow not shown.*

Instruments with Bodies Having No Corners: Guitar Shape (Type C)

C-1. Painting: *Madonna and Child*. Angel with vielle (showing characteristics of an early lira da braccio). Andrea del Verrocchio. Second half of 15th century. Hermitage, Leningrad. Pictured in *Basler Jahrbuch* VIII, p. 123 (detail). Four equidistant strings on fingerboard, one off; total of five strings on a curved bridge placed high between large inward-facing C-holes but close to tailpiece, which is also placed very high. Seven pegs shown. Ends of body not indented. Arched, short bow on strings at tip, far from bridge. Medium-size frog. Hand position on bow near end with first three fingers touching hair.

C-2. Painting: *Coronation of the Virgin*, showing four angels in the foreground, one playing an early form of the lira (or viola) da braccio, one lute, one recorder, and one presumably singing; in the background a group of nine musicians play various loud instruments, such as slide trumpets, bagpipe, and percussion. Zanobi Machiavelli, 1474. Museum, Dijon. Pictured in Winternitz, *Symbolism*, plate 68. Six equidistant strings all on fingerboard. Six pegs. Bridge appears to be flat, set below large C-holes, which face inward. Ends of body not indented. Highly arched, short, light bow on strings in lower part, far from bridge. Small frog. Hand position on bow away from end with second and third fingers touching hair.

C-3. Intarsia: lira da braccio with lute. Studio of Federigo da Montefeltre, Duke's palace, Urbino. Baccio Pontelli (ca. 1450-1492), ca. 1480. Pictured in MGG, vol. 8, plate 39-1; in Bowles, *Musikgeschichte,* p. 95; in Winternitz, *Leonardo,* p. 32, ex. 4.7; and in Winternitz, *Symbolism*, plate 52-a. Four equidistant strings on fingerboard plus one off. A slightly curved bridge is set high between large C-holes, which face inward. Five pegs. Ends of body not indented. No bow.

C-4. Bronze tomb for Sixtus IV: a lira (or viola) da braccio shown with other instruments, including positive organ, lute, percussion, and winds. Antonio Pollaiolo, 1493. St. Peters, Rome. Pictured in Bertelli, *Italian Renaissance Courts,* p. 122; in Capri, *Storia,* p. 237; and in Winternitz, *Leonardo*, p. 34, ex. 4.9. Four strings and four pegs. Bridge placement low between C-holes, which face inward. Bottom end of body indented. No bow.

C-5. Painting: *Ascension of Maria,* with detail showing an angel playing a lira da braccio, another playing a harp. Pietro Perugino, ca. 1500. Pitti Palace, Florence. Pictured in Geiser, *Studien,* no. 61 (detail); and in Sauerlandt, *Die Musik,* p. 36. Six strings, all on fingerboard with more space between third, fourth and fifth strings. Appear to be six pegs. Two lowest strings close together at bridge. The bridge appears to be curved and is placed low between the large C-holes, which face inward. Ends of body are not indented. Highly arched long bow on strings at tip, placed at a fairly normal playing distance from bridge. No frog. Hand position on bow at end.

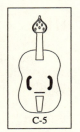
C-5

C-6. Engraving: a satyr playing a large lira da braccio in an exceptionally modern playing position. Jacopo de' Barbari, ca. 1500. Pictured in Hind, *Engravings*, vol. VII, plate 710, no. 19; and in Witten, "Apollo," p. 13, fig. 2 (detail). Five strings on fingerboard plus two off. Five pegs shown. Bridge appears to be slightly curved, set low between C-holes, which face inward. Bottom end of body unclear, top end not indented. Arched, medium-length bow on strings at middle, placed at normal distance from bridge. Frog not visible. Hand position on bow at end.

C-7. Woodcut: from *Morgante maggiore,* shows recitation with lira (or viola) da braccio. Luigi Pulci. Florence, 22.I.1500. Pictured in New Grove Dictionary, 1980, vol. 11, p. 21; and Witten, "Apollo," p. 13, fig. 3 (detail). Four (?) strings on fingerboard, none off, but five pegs. C-holes face inward. No bridge indicated. Body end indentation at bottom. Heavy, arched, long bow on strings in upper third. Small frog appears to be part of stick. Hand position on bow at end.

C-8. Painting: *Pan and Syrinx,* showing Pan playing a large lira da braccio. Pseudo-Boccaccino, ca. 1500. Thyssen-Bornemisza collection, cat. no. 32, Castagnola, near Lugano. Appear to be four strings on fingerboard. Bridge placed below C-holes, which face inward. Six (?) pegs placed laterally in a triangular pegbox. Lower end of body indented. Light, rather short, arched bow on strings at middle, set at normal distance from bridge. Frog unclear. Hand position on bow at end.*

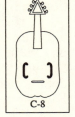
C-8

C-9. Painting: *Virgin on the Rocks,* with detail showing angel playing a lira da braccio. Ambrogio de Predis (Leonardo da Vinci), ca. 1500. National Gallery, London. Pictured in Geiser, *Studien,* no. 117; in Kinsky, *Geschichte,* p. 111, ill. 2; in MGG, vol. 8, plate 42-1; in Moreck, *Die Musik*, p. 20; in Sauerlandt, *Die Musik,* p. 54; in

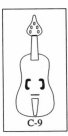

Winternitz, *Leonardo*, p. 68, exx. 5.31-5.32; and in Winternitz, *Symbolism*, plate 35-a. Equidistant strings with four on fingerboard, one off. Flat bridge set below C-holes, which face inward. Five pegs shown. Body ends are not indented. Slightly arched, short bow on strings in lower middle at some distance from the bridge. Medium-size frog. Hand position on bow at end.

C-10. Woodcut: poet with lira da braccio. Illustration from *Epithome Plutarchi* (Ferrara, 1501). Pictured in Kinsky, *Katalog*, p. 387; in MGG, vol. 8, p. 947; in New Grove Dictionary, vol. 11, p. 21; in Sander, *Le Livre*, no. 5772; in Winternitz, *Leonardo*, p. 37, ex. 4.12; in Winternitz, *Symbolism*, p. 94; and in Witten, "Apollo," p. 14, fig. 5 (detail). Four equidistant strings on fingerboard, two off, but eight pegs shown, one being on the side of the pegbox. C-holes are set high and face inward. No bridge shown. Ends of body not indented. Slightly arched, short bow separate from instrument. Medium-size frog appears to be part of stick.

C-11. Fresco: *Allegory of Music,* with woman playing a lira (or viola) da braccio on a throne flanked by players of flutes, harp, and a plucked instrument. Pinturicchio, 1455-1513. Pinacoteca Vaticana, Rome. Pictured in Capri, *Storia*, vol. 1, p. 263; in *Early Music,* vol. 10, no. 4 (October 1982), p. 439, fig. 26; in *Rassegna Musicale*, H. 8/9, 1928, plate 1; and in Sauerlandt, *Die Musik*, p. 41. Appear to be three strings on fingerboard and three pegs. Flat bridge (?) is placed low between C-holes, which face inward. Lower end of body appears to be indented, top end not indented. Arched, medium-length bow on strings at upper third, far from bridge. Frog unclear. Hand position on bow at end.

C-12. Painting: *The Madonna and Child with Four Musicians,* showing angels playing lira da braccio, lute, cornetto, and recorder. Attributed to Bernardino de Conti, ca. 1515-20. Location unknown since Christie's, London. Pictured in *Arte Cristiana,* Vol. 741, p. 409, no. 18. Appear to be three equidistant strings on fingerboard, but seven pegs indicated. Slightly curved bridge set somewhat low between inward-facing C-holes. Ends of body not indented. Arched, medium-length bow on strings at middle, far from bridge. Frog and hand position on bow unclear.

C-13. Woodcut: from *Historia de Apollonio di Tiro*, illustration of a recitation with lira da braccio. Florence, ca. 1515. Pictured in MGG, vol. 8, p. 951; in Winternitz, *Leonard*, p. 37, ex. 4.15; and in Witten, "Apollo," p. 15, fig. 6 (detail). Only two strings shown on fingerboard. Three pegs. C-holes face inward, placed high. Bridge not indicated. Lower end of body not visible, top end not indented. High arched, medium-length bow on strings at upper third. Frog unclear. Hand position on bow at end.

C-14. Woodcut: Frontispiece of Machiavelli, *Comedia di Callima*, depicting a centaur playing a lira (or viola) da braccio, ca. 1518. Pictured in Abbiati, *Storia*, p. 586; in *Early Music*, vol. 4, no. 3 (July 1976), p. 329. Three strings on fingerboard. Bridge set below S-shaped holes placed on upper bouts. Five pegs indicated. Body ends not indented. Long, arched bow on strings at upper third, far from bridge. Frog unclear. Hand position on bow at end.

C-15. Painting: *Ascension of Maria*, with detail showing an angel playing a lira da braccio and another playing lute. Giovanni di Benvenuto (1436-1518). Located in Montalcino. Pictured in MGG, vol. 8, p. 941. Seven equidistant strings on fingerboard. Flat bridge placed near tailpiece below C-holes, which face outward. Seven pegs. Ends of body not indented. Medium length, arched bow on strings in upper third at normal distance from bridge. No frog. Hand position on bow at end.

C-16. Woodcut: Title page of Lorenzo de' Medici (1492-1519), *Selve d'amore*. Lute player with lira (or viola) da braccio in background. Pictured in *Early Music*, vol. 3, no. 2 (April 1975) p. 138, no. 3; in MGG, vol. 8, p. 949; in Winternitz, *Leonardo*, p. 37, ex. 4.14; and in Winternitz, *Symbolism*, p. 96. Four equidistant strings shown on fingerboard. C-holes face inward. Other details unclear. Bottom end of body not indented but top end appears to be slightly indented. High arched, short bow separate from instrument. No frog.

C-17. Fresco: detail shows angel tuning a lira da braccio. Luca Signorelli (1441?-1523). Cathedral, Orvieto. Pictured in MGG, vol. 8, plate 41-2; and in Winternitz, *Symbolism*, plate 37-

b. Number of strings not visible. Other details not visible or unclear. At least five pegs are shown. Body ends not indented. No bow.

C-18. Fresco: *Coronation of the Virgin*. Detail shows an angel playing a lira da braccio with a metal ring on the thumb for stopping a string off the fingerboard. A lute player is shown on the left side of the picture. Girolamo del Pacchia (1477-after 1533). Chiesa di S. Spirito, Siena. Pictured in Disertori, "Pratica," pp. 164, 165 (details); and in *La pittura*, p. 336, no. 504. Four strings on fingerboard slightly grouped as 2+2, plus one off, closer to fourth string. A slightly curved bridge with three feet on the instrument is set below large C-holes, which face inward. Four upright pegs, one peg on the side. Top end of body indented but not bottom end. Medium arched bow of medium length with very large frog. Bow on strings near tip, far from bridge. Hand position on bow at end.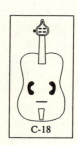

C-19. Fresco: *Concert of Angels*. Rare example of a lira da braccio being played on the lap in "gamba" position, appearing with over fifty other instruments. Gaudenzio Ferrari (1475-1546), 1534. Ceiling of the church of Santa Maria dei Miracoli, Saronno, Italy. Pictured in Bosseur, *Musique*, p. 22; and in Winternitz, *Leonardo*, p. 49, ex. 5.8. Number of strings unclear, but one off-the-fingerboard string visible. Six pegs. Flat bridge is placed low between reversed S-shaped sound holes. Top end of body indented, bottom not. Arched, short bow on strings at tip, at normal distance from bridge. Frog unclear. Bow held in underhand position at end.*

C-20. Painting: *Adoration of the Child,* showing youth playing a lira da braccio with lute and tromba marina players. Bartolomeo Suardi (Bramantino), fl. 1503-1536. Pinacoteca Ambrosiana, Milan. Strings and pegs unclear. Bridge set below C-holes, which face inward. Bottom end of body unclear, top end not indented. Arched bow, medium length, on strings near middle at normal distance from bridge. Frog not visible. Hand position on bow at end.*

C-21. Painting: *Adoration of the Magi,* with an angel tuning a lira da braccio, shown with other instruments. Eusebio da San Giorgio (active from 1465 or 70-1539). Pinacoteca Vannucci, Perugia. Pictured in Disertori, "Pratica," p. 156. View showing right side of instrument. Strings not visible. Four pegs visible from side view, which would indicate a total of seven. Other details not visible or unclear. Bottom end of body unclear, top end not indented. Arched, medium-length bow not totally visible, but probably on strings near tip. Large frog. Hand position on bow at end.

Instruments where Body Shapes Cannot Be Identified (Type D)

D-1. Painting: *Coronation of the Virgin*. Detail shows angels playing an early form of a lira da braccio and a portative organ. Gentile da Fabriano, 1390. Brera Palace, Milan. Pictured in MGG, vol. 8, plate 41-1; and in Winternitz, *Symbolism*, plate 35-b. Part of back visible, with seven pegs showing. Top end of body not indented. Only tip of arched bow visible.

D-2. Painting: *The Feast of the Gods*. A portion (upper bouts) of a lira da braccio shown, held by Apollo (Winternitz). Giovanni Bellini (1430-1516), also attributed to Dosso Dossi or Titian (*La pittura*). National Gallery, Washington, D.C. Pictured in Winternitz, *Symbolism*, plates 2 and 3-a (detail); and in *La pittura*, p. 261, no. 380. Five (?) strings on fingerboard plus two off. Top end of body not indented. Other details not visible. No bow.

D-3. Painting: Musician tuning lira da braccio. Raffaellino del Garbo (ca.1470-1524). National Gallery, Dublin. Pictured in Capri, *Storia*, p. 275 (attributed to Filippino Lippi); and in Winternitz, *Symbolism*, plate 32-b. Pegbox with five pegs, neck, one off-the-fingerboard string, and part of instrument's back show. Top end of body not indented. Upper part of bow visible, separate from instrument. Bow has exceptionally modern looking head.

D-4. Painting: Portrait of a musician tuning a lira da braccio. Domenico Mancini (?), ca. 1510. Kunsthistorisches Museum, Vienna. Pictured in H. Lützeler, *Musik*, p. 7 (attributed to Caravaggio). Five equidistant strings on fingerboard plus two off. Seven (?) lateral pegs. Top end of body not indented. Rare example of a lira da braccio with a sickle-shaped pegbox, ornamented, however, with a leaf. No bow.*

Instruments with Oval Body Shapes (Type E)

E-1. Engraving: *Apollo and Marsyas,* with a lira da braccio leaning upright against a rock, where Apollo is seated holding a bow. Marsyas shown playing a pan flute. Cristofano Robetta, ca. 1500-10. Pictured in Hind, *Engraving*, vol. III, plate 295. Back and side of instrument shown (reversed) with four equidistant strings indicated on bridge, plus one string off the fingerboard. Three pegs shown on leaf-shaped peg box, which would indicate two more on the far side, agreeing with the number of strings. Body ends not indented. High arched long bow. No frog. Hand position on bow at end.

The Iconography and Summary Charts

Iconography can reveal much information about the lira da braccio, but it must be observed with a great deal critical analysis. Such a variety of media--woodcuts, engravings, frescos, paintings, etc.--will differ greatly in the amount of informative detail one can obtain. This can range from only a suggestion of a line in a woodcut to an exact brush stroke of a fine painting. However, it is felt that all representations reveal something the artist saw or was familiar with to some degree and will thus reveal some aspect of reality. Not all details of an instrument will be shown in every example, but there will always be at least several that can be relied on. A woodcut can show in a rough way that a bridge is curved, whereas a shadow in a detailed painting may disguise this information completely. One is not able to see all or even any of the originals, so another great risk is the variety of clarity that exists when one must rely on reproductions. It is always best to try to compare two or more of the same picture. In the summary charts where only a guess about some detail is possible, an x in parentheses is used. The final numbers in the breakdown charts do not take these into account.

Each chart is accompanied by commentary, but in brief, the following are some conclusions drawn from the iconography and the few surviving instruments. All art examples except A-27, A-32, and A-33 were, if not of Italian origin, by Italian artists. Most information was obtained from paintings and woodcuts dating from the first third of the 16th century.[1] The subject matter was fairly equally divided between mythology, religion, and secular images. The player was invariably male with mythological subjects, an angel with religious subjects. The gender of an angel is often difficult to determine, but most angels would appear to be female in the selections presented here. Three main types of body shape were encountered, that of the violin form with four corners (type A), shapes with only two corners on the lower bouts (type B), and shapes with no corners, or guitar form, like that of the medieval fiddle (type C). One example of an oval-shaped instrument was found (E-1). Most of the instrument body shapes showed no end indentation; in those that did, the indentation is mainly at the bottom end. Most bridge placement was at the lower end of the sound holes, which in more than half of the examples were C-shaped holes facing inward. In about half of the examples the numbers of strings and pegs were not clear. The other half, in spite of mostly showing all the strings on the fingerboard, revealed a variety of combinations, most frequently five strings on the fingerboard and two alongside, seven pegs, and an equidistant arrangement of the strings. Bow characteristic had to be judged intuitively in relation to perspective and the size of the instruments. Most of them seemed to be medium to short arched bows with medium-size frogs, but some of the most true-to-life representations (B-5, B-6, B-22, C-5) showed long bows. About a third of the examples showed the bow away from the strings; in those shown in a playing position, the most frequent placement was in the middle or upper third of the bow, far from the bridge. Of those examples where the hand position on the bow could be clearly observed, about half were placed near or at the end of the bow; the other half were placed higher on the stick, and a few show some fingers touching the hair.

---

1. Where doubts about exact dating occur the latest possible date, namely the artist's death date (when known), was used.

LIRA DA BRACCIO INSTRUMENTS IN ICONOGRAPHY
Type A (four corners, or violin form). (x) = Unclear

Instrument no.		1	2	3	4	5	6	7	8	9	10	11	12	13	14	15	16	17	18	19	20	21	22	23	24	25	26	27	28	29	30	31	32	33	34	35	36	37	Totals
No. of strings on fingerboard	1																																						1
	2						(x)					x																											(1) 1
	3													x		x					x		x																4
	4															x		x				(x)		x				(x)			x	x	x		x				(2) 7
	5	x				x							x													x		x	x					x			x		8
	6							x																								x							2
	7										x																												1
	8																												x										1
Equidistant					x							x			x	x	x		x		x	x	x	x	x		(x)	x	x	x	x	x		x			x		(1) 17
Grouped		x						x		x														x									x		x				6
No. of strings off	1	x													x		(x)		(x)			x																	(2) 3
	2				x														x	(x)			x	(x)		x	x	x	x	x		x							(2) 9
	3																																						
Frets			x							x																				x									3
No. of pegs	3									x																													1
	4					x																																	1
	5														(x)			x	x			(x)																	(2) 2
	6	(x)						x																		x	(x)												(2) 2
	7			x			x			x	x							x			x			x	(x)		x	x											(1) 9
	8																																(x)						(1)
	9																				x																		1
Sound holes	( )	x	x	x	x	x	x	x		x	x		x	x				x		x																			13
	) (									x				x	x								x	x		x													6
	f																x		x		x			x			x	x	x		x								7
Placed:	S						x									x		x		x		x		x		x	x			x	x								9
High on table			x															x																					2
Low on table						x					x																												2
Bridge rel. to sound holes	Above				x																																		1
	High																																						
	Central																	x									x		x										3
	Low									x			x		x	x		x				x	x	x		x	x		x		x	x	x		x				13
	Below	x		x							x	x		x							x		x									x							8
Curved		x			x		x			x					x			x		x		x	x	x	(x)	x							x		x		x		(1) 11
Flat																														x		x							2
Body indent	Bottom	x					x		x			x	x							x	x	x		(x)								x	x						(1) 10
	Top	x														x			x			x																	4
	None	x	x		x	x	x	x	(x)	x		x		x	x		x	x	x		x		x	x	x		x	x	x			x	x						(1) 21
Mythology		x	x			x		x		x	x	x	x	x		x		x	x		x		x		x		x				x	x							17
Religious		x	x		x										x						x				x														5
Secular/Other				x		x		x		x					x		x		x		x					x	x	x	x	x	x			x	x			15
Player assoc.	Male	x	x	x			x		x	x	x	x	x	x	x	x	x		x		x	x	x	x		x	x	x	x	x	x		x		x	x		26
	Female					x													x																				2
	Angel	x		x										x																									3
	None						x											x						x	x	x		x	x										6
	Alone	x		x	x	x	x		x	x	x		x		x		x	x		x	x	x	x	x	x	x		x	x		x						22
With other instr.		x	x		x			x		x		x	x		x		x		x		x		x									x		x				14
End 15 c.		x																																					1
1st 3rd 16 c.		x	x	x	x	x	x	x	x	x	x	x	x	x	x	x	x																						15
2nd " "																		x	(x)	x	x																		(1) 3
3rd " "																						x	x	x	x	x	x	(x)	(x)	(x)	x	x							(3) 7
Begin 17 c.																														x	x	x	x	x	x	x	x	(x)	(1) 6
Intarsia							x																																1
Woodcut		x			x		x					x		x			x				x		x									x		x					10
Engraving		x						x		x		x			x						x		x			x	x			x									9
Painting				x		x				x				x	x	x		x		x		x		x			x		x				x					12
Drawing																		x	x		x			x			x									x			5
Watercolor																									x														1
Fresco																																							
Bronze			x																										x										2

This chart shows details for iconography of type A instruments (with four corners, or violin shape). This shape shows the widest spread within the time span of the lira da braccio, extending from the end of the 15th to the beginning of the 17th century. The most frequent string characteristics are four or five equidistant strings on the fingerboard with one or two off, most clearly shown toward the end of the 16th century. C-shaped sound holes facing inward predominated for the first third of the 16th century, with F- or S-shapes most common thereafter. The most common bridge placement is low or below the sound holes, with curved bridges more usual than flat ones. Most shapes are shown with no body end-indentation. Most examples are mythological and secular subjects found in woodcuts, engravings, and paintings.

LIRA DA BRACCIO INSTRUMENTS IN ICONOGRAPHY

Type B (instrument shapes with two corners). (x) = Unclear

Instrument no.		1	2	3	4	5	6	7	8	9	10	11	12	13	14	15	16	17	18	19	20	21	22	23	24	25	26	27	28	29	30	31	32	33	34		Totals
No. of strings on fingerboard	1			(x)																																	(1)
	2																																				
	3														x		x	x																			3
	4		x			x				x	x(x)		x											x		x		x		x			(x)				(2) 8
	5	x			x		(x)		x		x			x			x	x							x							x					(1) 8
	6																				x				x												2
	7														x																						1
	8																																				
Equidistant			x			x		x	x			x			x	x	x	x	x	x		x			x		x		x								13
Grouped		x			x						x		x											x		x			x								8
No. of strings off	1		x					(x)		x							x									x	x(x)		x								(2) 5
	2	x		x		x	x	x		x			x	x	x		x	x										x									12
	3																						x														1
Frets																								x		x											2
No. of pegs	3																																				
	4			(x)																																	(1)
	5	x							x										x		x																4
	6						(x)												x				x														(1) 2
	7	x			x	x		x			x	x(x)			x	x			x		x	x		x				x									(1) 12
	8																																				
	9													x																							1
Sound holes Placed:	( )	x	x	x	x	x	x	x	x		x	x	x	x	x	x	x	x	x	x	x	x	x	x	x			x			x	x	x				28
	) (																							x													1
	f																										x										1
	S							x																	x												2
High on table																			x		x																2
Low on table																			x		x		x	x													4
Bridge rel. to sound holes	Above																							x													1
	High															x																					1
	Central			x				(x)	x		x	x						x				x								x							(1) 7
	Low	x		x		x		(x)						x	x	x	x					x						x									(1) 9
	Below		x			x										x	x	x							x		x	x	x								9
Curved			x		x		(x)		x			x	x	x	x	x	x				x	x	x			x				x(x)	x						(2) 15
Flat		x														x										x											3
Body indent	Bottom											x		x									x														3
	Top	x											x	x									x														4
	None		x	x			x	(x)	x	x	x	x	x	x(x)		x			x			x		x	x	x	x		x	x	x	x	x				(2) 21
Mythology							x						x	x				x	x					x	x			x	x								9
Religious			x		x		x	x	x		x	x				x	x	x		x	x	x				x	x					x	x				17
Secular/Other		x		x	x				x					x							x	x				x											8
Player association	Male		x		x		x			x		x	x			x					x	x	x	x		(x)	x	x	x							(1) 17
	Female																																				
	Angel			x		x	x	x	x		x	x				x			x	x	x					x				x						12
	None	x	x											x						x						x										4
	Alone	x	x		x		x				x		x				x			x		x	x	x			x								11
With other instr.			x	x	x		x		(x)	x		x		x	x		x	x			x	x		x					x	x			x			(1) 16
End 15 c.		x	x	x																																	3
1st 3rd 16 c.					x	x	x	x	x	x	x	x	x	x	x	x(x)	x	x	x	x	x	x	x	x	x	x	x	x	x(x)							(2) 25
2nd " "																											x(x)	x	(x)							(2) 2
3rd " "																																				
Begin 17 c.																																				
Intarsia				x												x																				2
Woodcut		x	x											x			x	x	x			x	x	x			x							11
Engraving							x																														1
Painting				x	x		x	x	x	x	x	x		x						x	x	x				x	x	x	x	x		x				18
Drawing															x							x														2
Watercolor																																				
Fresco														x																						1
Bronze																																				

This chart shows details for iconography of type B instruments (with two corners). This shape appears mostly within the first third of the 16th century and is seen most often in religious paintings. Woodcuts show this shape mainly with secular and mythological subjects. The most frequent string characteristics are four or five equidistant strings on the fingerboard, with one or two off. C-shape sound holes are the most common with this instrument shape. Bridge placement low or below the sound holes is the most frequent, with some centrally located. Most bridges show a curve, if often only slightly. More instruments are shown with no body end-indentation than with. For theories on this instrument shape, see Winternitz, *Leonardo*, pp. 39-72.

LIRA DA BRACCIO INSTRUMENTS IN ICONOGRAPHY
Type C (no corners, or guitar form). (x) = Unclear

Instrument no.	1	2	3	4	5	6	7	8	9	10	11	12	13	14	15	16	17	18	19	20	21	Totals
No. of strings on fingerboard 1													x									1
2												x										1
3											x	x		x								3
4	x		x	x			(x)	(x)	x	x					x		x					(2) 7
5						x																1
6		x			x																	2
7														x								1
8																						
Equidistant	x	x	x						x	x	x	x			x	x						9
Grouped					x											x						2
No. of strings off 1	x		x					x								x	x					5
2					x					x												2
3																						1
Frets																						
No. of pegs 3											x		x									2
4				x																		1
5			x				x	x		x					x		x					(1) 6
6		x							(x)								x					(1) 3
7	x										x			x						(x)		(1) 3
8										x												1
9																						
Sound holes ( )	x	x	x	x	x	x	x	x	x	x	x	x	x			x		x		x		16
)(															x							1
f																						
S																						
Placed: High on table															x			x				2
Low on table											x		x	x								3
Bridge rel. to sound holes: Above																						
High	x	x																				2
Central																						
Low			x	x	x						x	x					x					6
Below		x						x	x					x	x		x		x			7
Curved	x		x		x	x						x					x					6
Flat		x						x		(x)				x			x					(1) 4
Body indent: Bottom			x			x	x				x											4
Top															x		x	x				3
None	x	x	x		x				x	x		x		x	x		x					10
Mythology					x		x						x									3
Religious	x	x		x	x			x			x				x	x	x	x	x		x	12
Secular/Other			x			x			x	x			x									6
Player assoc-iation: Male					x	x	x					x	x						x			7
Female										x												1
Angel	x	x			x			x			x				x	x	x	x			x	10
None			x	x										x								3
Alone						x	x		x					x	x							5
With other instr.		x	x	x	x						x	x			x	x		x	x	x	x	12
End 15 c.	x	x	x	x																		4
1st 3rd 16 c.					x	x	x	x	x	x	x	x	x	x	x	x	x	x				14
2nd " "																		x	(x)	(x)		(2) 1
3rd " "																						
Begin 17 c.																						
Intarsia		x																				1
Woodcut						x			x				x	x			x					5
Engraving					x																	1
Painting	x	x			x			x	x				x		x					x	x	9
Drawing																						
Watercolor																						
Fresco											x	x				x	x	x				4
Bronze			x																			1

This chart shows details for iconography of type C intruments (no corners or guitar shape). Instruments of this shape appear in the iconography at the end of the 15th century and continue to appear through the first third of the 16th century. Fewer examples of this shape occur. Four mainly equidistant strings on the fingerboard with one or two strings off are the most frequent string combinations, confirmed by the five pegs usually seen. More instruments appear without body end-indentation than with. C-shaped sound holes facing inward predominate with this shape. Instruments of this type appear frequently in paintings and frescos of religious subjects, and to some extent in woodcuts dealing with secular and mythological subjects.

LIRA DA BRACCIO INSTRUMENTS IN ICONOGRAPHY

Type D (total shapes not visible). Type E (oval shape). Extant Instruments Type A / Type B / Type: A B C D E Totals

(x) = Unclear or not original

	D 1	D 2	D 3	D 4	D Tot	E 1	E Tot	A 1	A 2	A 3	A 4	A 5	A 6	A 8	A 9	A Tot	B 7	B 10	B Tot	A 45	B 36	C 21	D 4	E 1	Tot 107
No. of strings on fingerboard 1																				(1)					(1)
2																				(1)	1	1			(1)2.
3																				4	3	3			10
4						x	1													(2)7	(2)8	(2)7		1	(6)23
5	(x)		x	(1)	1			x	x	(x)	(x)	x	(x)	(x)	(x)	(4)3				8	(1)8		1	(1)1	(6)21
6																				2	2	2			6
7																				1	1	1			3
8																				1					1
Equidistant			x		1	x	1	x		(x)	(x)	x	(x)			(3)2	x		1	(1)17	13	9	1	1	(4)43
Grouped								x								1				6	8	2			17
No. of strings off 1		x			1	x	1													(2)3	(2)5	5	1	1	(4)15
2	x		x		2			x	x	(x)	(x)	x	(x)	(x)		(4)3				(2)9	12	2	2		(6)28
3																									1
Frets																				3	2				5
No. of pegs 3																				1		2			3
4																				1	(1)	1			(1)2
5			x		1	(x)(1)		x	x	(x)	(x)	x	(x)	(x)		(4)3				(2)2	4	(1)6	1	(1)	(4)13
6																				(2)2	(1)2	(1)3			(4)7
7	x		(x)	(1)	1			x	x	(x)	(x)	x	(x)	(x)		(4)3				(1)9	(1)12	(1)3	(1)1		(8)28
8																				(1)		1			(1)1
9																				1	1				2
Sound holes C))(														x		1	x		1	13	28	16			59
f																				6	1	1			8
S / **Placed:**								x	x		x					3	x		1	7	1				12
High on table											x	x	x	x		4				9	2	2			17
Low on table																				2	2	3			7
																				2	4				6
Bridge rel. to sound holes: Above																					1				1
High																				1	1	2			4
Central								x	x	(x)(x)		x	(x)(x)			(4)3				3	(1)7				(5)13
Low																				13	(1)9	6			(1)28
Below																				8	9	7			24
Curved								x	x	(x)(x)		x	(x)(x)			(4)3				(1)11	(2)15	6			(7)35
Flat																				2	3	(1)4			(1)9
Body indent Bottom								x	x	x	x	x	x	x	x	8	x	x	2	(1)10	3	4			(1)27
Top									x							1				4	4	3			12
None						x	1													(1)21	(2)21	10		1	(3)53
Mythology		x			1	x	1													17	9	3	1	1	31
Religious	x				1															5	17	12	1		35
Secular/Other			x	x	2															15	8	6	2		31
Player assoc. Male		x	x	x	3	x	1													26	(1)17	7	3	1	(1)54
Female																				2		1			3
Angel	x				1															3	12	10	1		26
None																				6	4	3			13
Alone		x	x	x	3															22	11	5	3		41
With other instr.	x				1	x	1													14	(1)16	12	1	1	(1)
End 15 c.	x				1															1	3	4	1		9
1st 3rd 16 c.	(x)	(x)	x	(2)		x	1				x					1				15	(2)25	14	(2)1	1	(4)57
2nd " "						x	1				x					1				(1)3	(2)2	(2)1			(5)7
3rd " "								(x)			x					(1)1	(x)	x	(1)1	(3)7					(5)9
Begin 17 c.																				(1)6					(1)6
Intarsia																				1	2	1			4
Woodcut																				10	11	5			26
Engraving						x	1													9	1	1		1	12
Painting	x	x	x	x	4															12	18	9	4		43
Drawing																				5	2				7
Watercolor																				1					1
Fresco																					1	4			5
Bronze																				2		1			3

This chart shows details for iconography of type D instruments (total shapes not visible), of type E (oval shape), of extant instruments, and totals for all iconography types and extants combined. All extant original instruments as well as those restored show five strings on the fingerboard and two strings off. All show body end-indentation. Only two have C-shaped sound holes, the others having F- or S-shaped holes. Eight are type A, with four corners, or violin shape, and two are of type B, with only two corners. The overall totals show mostly four or five strings on the fingerboard and mostly two strings off. C-shaped sound holes facing inward predominate, especially during the first third of the 16th century. Clear examples show bridges with some curve. In contrast to the extant instruments, most instrument shapes show no body end-indentation in the iconography, but if so then at the bottom end. Subject matter in the iconography is equally divided between mythological, religious, and secular subjects, with instruments being held or played mainly by male figures. Over half of the examples date within the first third of the 16th century. Most examples appear in paintings, but many are in woodcuts and engravings.

LIRA DA BRACCIO: NUMBER OF STRINGS

Total of 107 examples: 97 in iconography and 10 extant instruments. ☐ = Agree with no. of pegs.   (x) Probable but not counted.

Type A (four corners, or violin form).

Number of strings	Instr. 1–37	Summary
2	x (at 11)	1
3	x (13) x (15) x (20) x (22)	4
4	x (14) x (31)	2
5	x (9) x (16)	2
6	x (1) ☐(6) ☐(10) x (24) x x (28 29) x (31)	6
7	☐(5) ☐(11) ☐(29) ☐(33) x (36)	5
8	x (34)	1
9	☐(25)	1
?	x x x (3 4 5) x x x (7 8 9) x (13) x x (16 17) x (19) x (22) x x (24 25) x (27) x (36)	15

Extants 1–10

| 7 | x x (1 2) ☐(5) | 3 |
| ? | x x (3 4) x (6) x x (8 9) | 5 (2) |

Totals for A: 1 4 2 2 6 8 1 1 20

Type B (two corners).

Number of strings	Instr. 1–34	Summary
3	x (18) x (20)	2
4	x (14) x (22) x (24)	3
5	☐(3) x (12) x (25) x (30) (x)(32)	4
6	x (11) ☐(17) x (23)	3
7	x (1) ☐(6) ☐(10) ☐(13) x x (18 19) ☐(25) ☐(31)	8
8		
9	☐(13)	1
?	x x (3 4) x x x (6 7 8) ☐(11) x x (18 19) x x (25 26) x (29) x (32)	13

Extants 1–10

| ? | x (5) x (7) | 2 |

Totals for B: 2 3 4 3 8 1 15

Type C (no corners, or guitar form).

Number of strings	Instr. 1–21	Summary
2	x (11)	1
3	x x (9 10) x (12)	3
4	☐(4) x (13)	2
5	x (1) ☐(3) ☐(10) ☐(16)	4
6	☐(2) ☐(4) x (8)	3
7	x (6) ☐(13)	2
?	x x (7 8) x (16) x x x (18 19 20)	6

D (total shapes not visible).

Number of strings	Instr. 1 2 3 4	Summary
7	☐(4)	1
?	x x x (1 2 3)	3

E (oval shape).

Number of strings	Instr. 1	Summary
5	x	1

Totals for all:

Number of strings		
2	2	
3	9	
4	7	
5	11	
6	12	
7	19	
8	1	
9	2	
?	44	

26 agree with number of pegs in iconography.

This chart shows the number of strings shown on liras da braccio in the iconographical examples and on extant instruments. Of the 97 iconographical examples, 60 are clear enough to determine the number of strings. Sixteen show seven strings, thirteen of which are confirmed by the number of pegs shown. Twelve show six strings, with four confirmed by the number of pegs; eleven show five strings, with five confirmed by the pegs shown. These represent the most likely possibilities in reality, with seven strings being the most common on lira da braccio instruments. In all, 26 show the same number of strings and pegs (see appropriate charts). Only three extant instruments have their original necks and pegboxes verifying the number of seven strings.

LIRA DA BRACCIO: STRING PLACEMENT

Total of 107 examples: 97 in iconography and 10 extant instruments.

Type A (four corners, or violin form).

Instrument no.	1	2	3	4	5	6	7	8	9	10	11	12	13	14	15	16	17	18	19	20	21	22	23	24	25	26	27	28	29	30	31	32	33	34	35	36	37	Summary
Equidistant					x							x		x	x		x				x	x	x	x		x			x	x	x	x	x		x		x	17
Some grouping	x							x		x														x									x		x			6
Unclear		x	x	x		x	x	x		x			x			x		x	x						x	x										x		14

Extants	1	2	3	4	5	6	7	8	9	10			Summary
Equidistant	x			x									2
Some grouping		x											1
Unclear			x	x		x		x	x				5

Totals for A: 19 | 7 | 19

Type B (two corners).

Instrument no.	1	2	3	4	5	6	7	8	9	10	11	12	13	14	15	16	17	18	19	20	21	22	23	24	25	26	27	28	29	30	31	32	33	34	Summary
Equidistant		x				x			x	x			x		x	x	x	x	x	x				x		x									13
Some grouping	x			x								x		x								x	x		x				x						8
Unclear			x		x		x	x			x										x	x				x	x				x	x	x	x	13

Extants	1	2	3	4	5	6	7	8	9	10		Summary
Unclear							x		x			2

Totals for B: 13 | 8 | 15

Type C (no corners, or guitar form).

Instrument no.	1	2	3	4	5	6	7	8	9	10	11	12	13	14	15	16	17	18	19	20	21	Summary
Equidistant	x	x	x					x	x	x	x			x	x							9
Some grouping					x												x					2
Unclear			x		x	x	x					x	x			x		x	x	x		10

D (total shapes not visible).

Instrument no.	1	2	3	4	Summary
Equidistant			x		1
Some grouping					
Unclear	x	x	x		3

E (oval shape).

Instrument no.	1	Summary
Equidistant	x	1
Some grouping		
Unclear		

Totals for all:		
Equidistant	43	
Some grouping	17	
Unclear		47

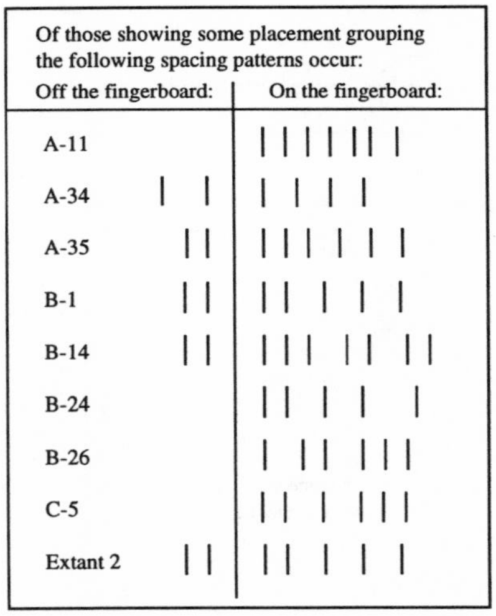

Of those showing some placement grouping the following spacing patterns occur:

	Off the fingerboard:	On the fingerboard:
A-11		| | | | || |
A-34	| |	| | | |
A-35	||	| | || | |
B-1	||	| | | | |
B-14	||	||| || ||
B-24		| | | | |
B-26	|	| || |||
C-5	||	|| | |||
Extant 2	||	|| | | |

This chart shows string placement shown on liras da braccio in the iconographical examples and on extant instruments. Of the 97 iconographical examples, 57 are clear enough to determine string characteristics. Forty-one show equidistant strings, and sixteen show some grouping. One extant instrument shows some grouping, as shown in the chart above.

LIRA DA BRACCIO: STRING COMBINATIONS

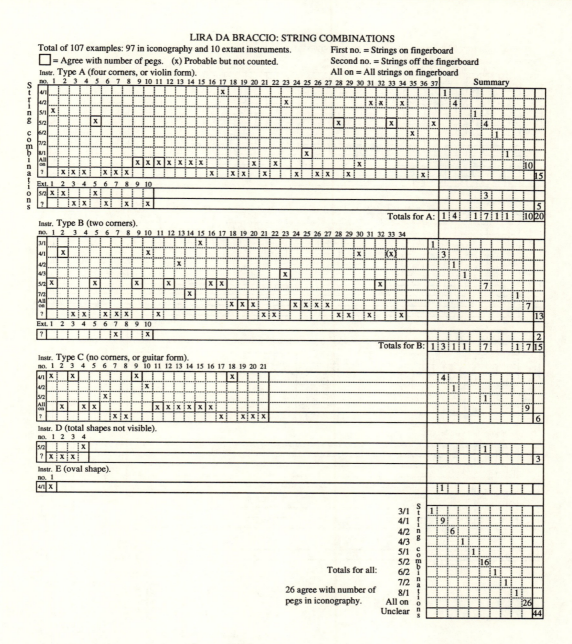

Total of 107 examples: 97 in iconography and 10 extant instruments.　　First no. = Strings on fingerboard

☐ = Agree with number of pegs.　(x) Probable but not counted.　Second no. = Strings off the fingerboard

All on = All strings on fingerboard

Totals for all:

26 agree with number of pegs in iconography.

This chart shows the various on- and off-the-fingerboard string combinations on liras da braccio shown in the iconografical examples and on extant instruments. Of the 60 iconographical examples where string combinations are clearly visible, 26 show all the strings on the fingerboard, these being almost entirely within the first third of the 16th century. Of the remaining combinations the most frequent are five strings on the fingerboard with two off (thirteen examples) and four strings on the fingerboard with one off (nine examples). Twenty-six examples agree with the number of pegs shown (see next chart). One example (B-23) shows three strings off the fingerboard. Only three extant instruments are in their original condition, these having five strings on the fingerboard and two off.

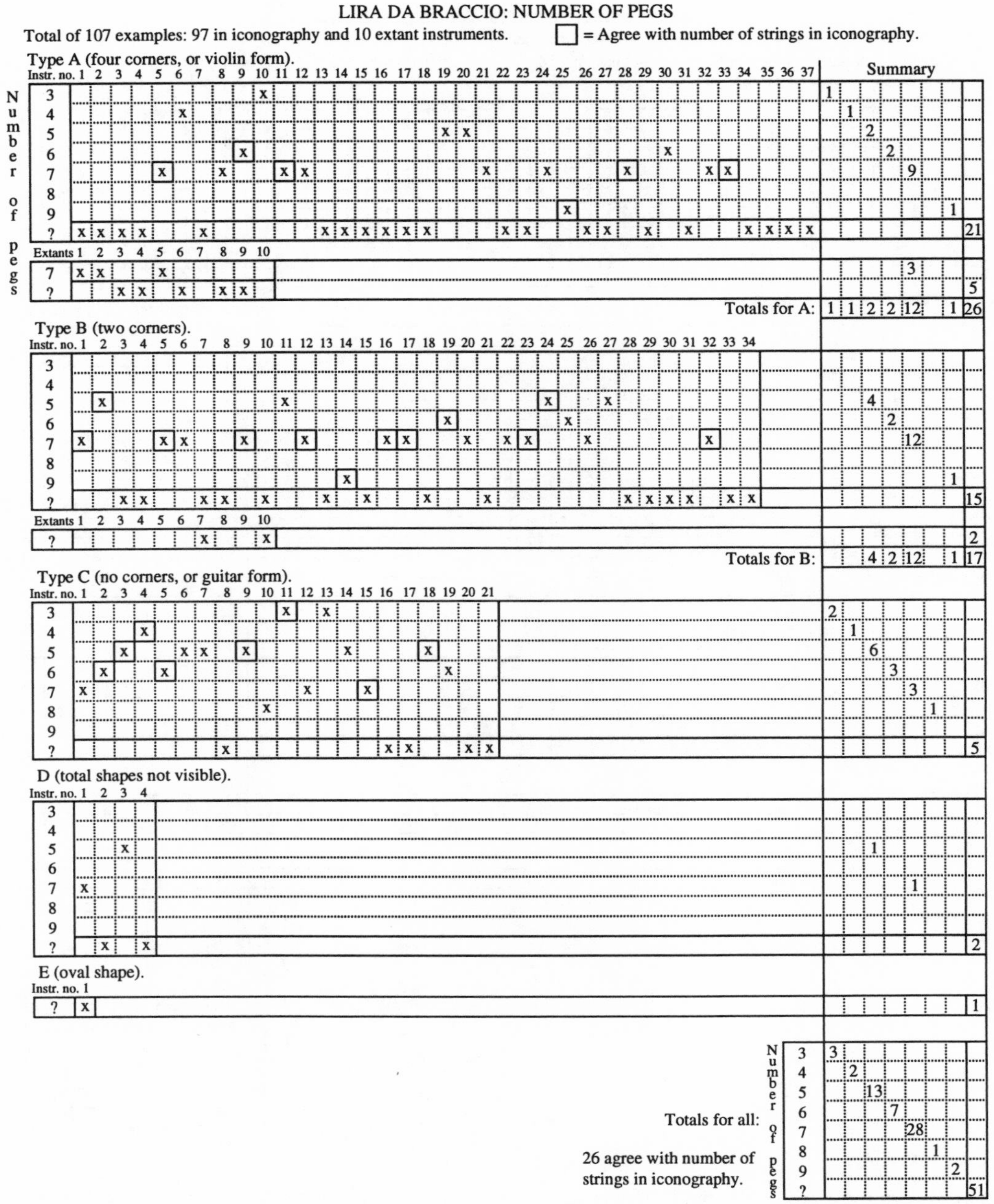

LIRA DA BRACCIO: NUMBER OF PEGS

Total of 107 examples: 97 in iconography and 10 extant instruments.   ☐ = Agree with number of strings in iconography.

Type A (four corners, or violin form).
Instr. no. 1 2 3 4 5 6 7 8 9 10 11 12 13 14 15 16 17 18 19 20 21 22 23 24 25 26 27 28 29 30 31 32 33 34 35 36 37   Summary

Number of pegs:

pegs	marks	Summary
3	x (at 10)	1
4	x (at 5)	1
5	x x (at 19, 20)	2
6	x (at 7), x (at 30)	2
7	x x x x x x x x x	9
8		
9	x (at 25)	1
?	x x x x x x x x x x x x x x x x x x x x x	21

Extants 1 2 3 4 5 6 7 8 9 10

pegs	marks	Summary
7	x x x	3
?	x x x x x	5

Totals for A: 1 1 2 2 12 1 26

Type B (two corners).
Instr. no. 1 2 3 4 5 6 7 8 9 10 11 12 13 14 15 16 17 18 19 20 21 22 23 24 25 26 27 28 29 30 31 32 33 34

pegs	Summary
3	
4	
5	4
6	2
7	12
8	
9	1
?	15

Extants 1 2 3 4 5 6 7 8 9 10

pegs	Summary
?	2

Totals for B: 4 2 12 1 17

Type C (no corners, or guitar form).
Instr. no. 1 2 3 4 5 6 7 8 9 10 11 12 13 14 15 16 17 18 19 20 21

pegs	Summary
3	2
4	1
5	6
6	3
7	3
8	1
9	
?	5

D (total shapes not visible).
Instr. no. 1 2 3 4

pegs	Summary
3	
4	
5	1
6	
7	1
8	
9	
?	2

E (oval shape).
Instr. no. 1

pegs	Summary
?	1

Totals for all:

Number of pegs	
3	3
4	2
5	13
6	7
7	28
8	1
9	2
?	51

26 agree with number of strings in iconography.

This chart shows the number of pegs shown on liras da braccio in the iconographical examples and on extant instruments. Of the 53 examples in the iconography which clearly show the number of pegs, 25 show the usual seven, thirteen show five pegs, and seven show six pegs. Only three extant instruments are in their original condition, these having seven pegs. About half of the examples (26) in the iconography agree with the number of strings shown (see previous chart).

LIRA DA BRACCIO: BRIDGES (relation to sound holes)

Total of 107 examples: 97 in iconography and 10 extant instruments. (x) = Probable but not counted.

Type A (four corners, or violin form).

Instr. no. 1 2 3 4 5 6 7 8 9 10 11 12 13 14 15 16 17 18 19 20 21 22 23 24 25 26 27 28 29 30 31 32 33 34 35 36 37

Position/Shape	Instruments marked (x)	Summary
Above		
High	5	1
Central	19, 29, 32	3
Low	6, 10, 11, 13, 22, 23, 24, 27, 28, 31, 33, 34, 36	13
Below	1, 3, 8, 9, 12, 19, 23, 35	8
Curved	1, 3, 5, 16, 21, 23, 24, 25, 28, 33, 35	11
Flat	31, 33	2
Unclear or none*	1, 3, 6, 7, 9, 12, 16, 18, 19, 26, 29, 30	12

Extants 1 2 3 4 5 6 7 8 9 10

Position/Shape	Extants marked (x)	Summary
Central	1, 2, 4	3
Curved	1, 2, 4	3
Unclear	3, 4, 6, 8, 9	5

Totals for A: 1 6 13 8 14 2 17

Type B (two corners).

Instr. no. 1 2 3 4 5 6 7 8 9 10 11 12 13 14 15 16 17 18 19 20 21 22 23 24 25 26 27 28 29 30 31 32 33 34

Position/Shape	Instruments marked (x)	Summary
Above	24	1
High	18	1
Central	4, 9, 11, 12, 17, 23, 30	7
Low	1, 3, 4, 13, 14, 15, 16, 21, 22, 30	9
Below	2, 5, 19, 20, 25, 27, 28, 29	9
Curved	2, 4, 8, 12, 13, 14, 15, 16, 17, 21, 22, 23, 26, 29, 31	15
Flat	1, 18, 27	3
Unclear or none*	24, 25, 27, 33	7

Extants 1 2 3 4 5 6 7 8 9 10

Position/Shape	Extants marked (x)	Summary
Unclear	6, 8	2

Totals for B: 1 1 7 9 9 15 3 9

Type C (no corners, or guitar form).

Instr. no. 1 2 3 4 5 6 7 8 9 10 11 12 13 14 15 16 17 18 19 20 21

Position/Shape	Instruments marked (x)	Summary
Above		
High	1, 3	2
Central		
Low	4, 5, 6, 10, 11, 17	6
Below	2, 7, 8, 12, 13, 16, 18	7
Curved	1, 2, 4, 5, 10, 17	6
Flat	2, 9(x), 13, 16	4
Unclear or none*	6, 9, 12, 15, 16, 19	6

D (total shapes not visible).

Instr. no. 1 2 3 4

Position/Shape	Instruments marked (x)	Summary
Unclear	1, 2, 3, 4	4

E (oval shape).

Instr. no. 1

Position/Shape	Instruments marked (x)	Summary
Unclear	1	1

Totals for all:

Above	1
High	4
Central	13
Low	28
Below	24
Curved	35
Flat	9
Unclear or none*	37

x* No bridge = 7

This chart shows the positions and characteristics of bridges on liras da braccio in the iconographical examples and on extant instruments. Of the 67 examples where bridges are visible in the iconography, the placement is low between the sound holes in 28 examples, placement is below the sound holes in 24 examples, and placement is central in ten examples. Seven examples clearly show no bridges at all. Out of 40 examples where bridge shapes can be clearly observed, 32 show various degrees of curvature and nine appear to be flat. The three extant instruments in their original state have curved bridges placed centrally, or nearly so, between the sound holes. However, these may not have been their original positions and shapes. One of these three may still have its original bridge (see extant no. 5).

LIRA DA BRACCIO: SOUND HOLES

Total of 107 examples: 97 in iconography and 10 extant instruments.

Type A (four corners, or violin form).

Instr. no. 1 2 3 4 5 6 7 8 9 10 11 12 13 14 15 16 17 18 19 20 21 22 23 24 25 26 27 28 29 30 31 32 33 34 35 36 37 | Summary

	1	2	3	4	5	6	7	8	9	10	11	12	13	14	15	16	17	18	19	20	21	22	23	24	25	26	27	28	29	30	31	32	33	34	35	36	37	Summary
( )	x	x	x	x	x	x	x		x	x		x	x						x		x																	13
) (											x			x	x									x	x		x											6
ƒ																		x		x			x			x			x	x	x		x					7
S				x											x		x				x			x				x	x			x	x					9
High	x															x																						2
Low				x								x																										2
Unclear														x		x																						2

Extants 1 2 3 4 5 6 7 8 9 10

	1	2	3	4	5	6	7	8	9	10	Summary
( )				x							1
) (											
ƒ	x	x		x							3
S		x			x		x	x			4
High											
Low											

Totals for A: 14 6 10 13 2 2 2

Type B (two corners).

Instr no. 1 2 3 4 5 6 7 8 9 10 11 12 13 14 15 16 17 18 19 20 21 22 23 24 25 26 27 28 29 30 31 32 33 34 | Summary

	1	2	3	4	5	6	7	8	9	10	11	12	13	14	15	16	17	18	19	20	21	22	23	24	25	26	27	28	29	30	31	32	33	34	Summary
( )	x	x	x	x	x	x	x	x	x	x		x	x	x	x	x	x	x	x	x	x	x	x	x	x		x			x	x	x			28
) (																										x									1
ƒ																									x										1
S										x																									2
High																	x				x												2		2
Low												x		x				x	x														4		4
Unclear																													x					x	2

Extants 1 2 3 4 5 6 7 8 9 10

	1	2	3	4	5	6	7	8	9	10	Summary
( )										x	1
) (											
ƒ							x				1
S											
High											
Low											

Totals for B: 29 1 2 2 2 4 2

Type C (no corners, or guitar form).

Instr. no. 1 2 3 4 5 6 7 8 9 10 11 12 13 14 15 16 17 18 19 20 21 | Summary

	1	2	3	4	5	6	7	8	9	10	11	12	13	14	15	16	17	18	19	20	21	Summary
( )	x	x	x	x	x	x	x	x	x	x	x	x	x			x		x		x		16
) (													x									1
ƒ																						
S											x				x							2
High										x			x	x								3
Low																						
Unclear														x			x					2

D (total shapes not visible).

Instr. no. 1 2 3 4

	1	2	3	4						Summary
Unclear	x	x	x	x						4

E (oval shape).

Instr. no. 1

	1									Summary
Unclear	x									1

Totals for all:

( )	59	
) (	8	
ƒ		12
S		17
High		7
Low		6
Unclear		11

This chart shows the types and positions of sound holes on liras da braccio in the iconographical examples and on extant instruments. Of the 86 clear examples in the iconography, 65 have C-shaped sound holes, of which 57 face inward and eight face outward; thirteen have S-shaped and eight have F-shaped sound holes. Since most of these examples date from the first third of the 16th century, the early C-shaped sound hole is seen most frequently, the form most commonly seen on medieval fiddles as well. F-shaped sound hole are seen mostly on type A instruments (this type having the longest time span), but not before the last third of the 16th century, the S-shape form being most common earlier. Of the ten extant instruments, five have F-shaped, three have S-shaped, and two have C-shaped sound holes.

LIRA DA BRACCIO: BODY SHAPES

Total of 107 examples: 97 in iconography and 10 extant instruments.

Type A (four corners, or violin form).

Instrument no.	1	2	3	4	5	6	7	8	9	10	11	12	13	14	15	16	17	18	19	20	21	22	23	24	25	26	27	28	29	30	31	32	33	34	35	36	37	Summary
No indentation	x			x	x	x	x		x		x		x	x					x	x	x			x		x	x	x		x	x	x				x	x	21
Bottom indent.								x		x					x	x						x	x										x	x				8
Top end indent.																	x								x													2
Both ends indent.			x																		x																	2
Unclear							x									x		x											x									4

Extants	1	2	3	4	5	6	7	8	9	10									Summary
No indentation																			
Bottom indent.	x	x	x	x		x		x	x										7
Top end indent.																			
Both ends indent.					x														1
Unclear																			

Totals for A: 21 | 15 | 2 | 3 | 4

Type B (two corners).

Instrument no.	1	2	3	4	5	6	7	8	9	10	11	12	13	14	15	16	17	18	19	20	21	22	23	24	25	26	27	28	29	30	31	32	33	34	Summary
No indentation		x	x			x		x	x	x	x	x		x				x					x	x	x	x	x	x		x	x	x	x	x	21
Bottom indent.														x		x																			2
Top end indent.	x																x	x																	3
Both ends indent.																													x						1
Unclear				x	x		x						x							x	x	x													7

Extants	1	2	3	4	5	6	7	8	9	10								Summary
No indentation																		
Bottom indent.				x			x											2
Top end indent.																		
Both ends indent.																		
Unclear																		

Totals for B: 21 | 4 | 3 | 1 | 7

Type C (no corners, or guitar form).

Instrument no.	1	2	3	4	5	6	7	8	9	10	11	12	13	14	15	16	17	18	19	20	21	Summary
No indentation	x	x	x		x		x	x		x		x	x		x							10
Bottom indent.			x			x	x		x													4
Top end indent.														x		x	x					3
Both ends indent.																						
Unclear				x					x								x	x				4

D (total shapes not visible).

Instrument no.	1	2	3	4	Summary
No indentation					
Bottom indent.					
Top end indent.					
Both ends indent.					
Unclear	x	x	x	x	4

E (oval shape).

Instrument no.	1	Summary
No indentation	x	1

Totals for all:

	Summary
No indentation	53
Bottom indent.	23
Top end indent.	8
Both ends indent.	4
Unclear	19

This chart shows the body shape features of liras da braccio in the iconographical examples and of extant instruments. Out of 78 examples in the iconography where body shapes can be seen, 53 show no end indentation, fourteen show indentation at the bottom end where the tailpiece is attached, eight show indentation at the top where the neck joins the body, and three show indentation at both ends. There is no correlation between body end indentation features and dates of the examples. All ten extant instruments have body end-indentation at the bottom, with one having indentation at both ends.

LIRA DA BRACCIO: SUBJECT MATTER IN ICONOGRAPHY

Total of 97 examples.

Type A (four corners, or violin form).

Instrument no.	1	2	3	4	5	6	7	8	9	10	11	12	13	14	15	16	17	18	19	20	21	22	23	24	25	26	27	28	29	30	31	32	33	34	35	36	3	Summary
Mythology	x		x			x		x		x	x	x	x			x		x	x			x		x		x		x							x	x		17
Religious		x			x												x						x				x											5
Secular				x		x		x		x				x			x			x		x		x		x			x	x	x	x	x	x				15

Type B (two corners).

Instrument no.	1	2	3	4	5	6	7	8	9	10	11	12	13	14	15	16	17	18	19	20	21	22	23	24	25	26	27	28	29	30	31	32	33	34	Summary
Mythology						x						x	x					x	x					x	x			x	x						9
Religious		x		x		x	x	x		x	x				x	x	x		x	x	x					x	x			x	x				17
Secular	x		x	x						x				x								x	x					x							8

Type C (no corners, or guitar form).

Instrument no.	1	2	3	4	5	6	7	8	9	10	11	12	13	14	15	16	17	18	19	20	21	Summary
Mythology					x		x					x										3
Religious	x	x		x	x			x		x			x		x	x	x	x	x			12
Secular			x			x			x	x		x			x							6

D (total shapes not visible).

Instrument no.	1	2	3	4	Summary
Mythology		x			1
Religious	x				1
Secular			x	x	2

E (oval shape).

Instrument no.	1	Summary
Mythology	x	1

Totals for all:		
Mythology	31	
Religious	35	
Secular	31	

This chart shows the subject matter of the iconographical examples where liras da braccio appear. It shows an almost equal division between mythological, religious, and secular subjects over the historical time span of the lira da braccio.

LIRA DA BRACCIO: PLAYER ASSOCIATION IN ICONOGRAPHY

Total of 97 examples.   (x) = Probable but not counted.

Type A (four corners, or violin form).

Instrument no.	1	2	3	4	5	6	7	8	9	10	11	12	13	14	15	16	17	18	19	20	21	22	23	24	25	26	27	28	29	30	31	32	33	34	35	36	37	Summary
Male	x		x	x			x		x	x	x	x	x	x	x		x			x	x	x	x		x	x	x	x	x	x			x			x	x	26
Female					x														x																			2
Angel		x			x											x																						3
None						x																			x					x	x	x	x					6
Alone		x		x	x	x		x	x		x			x		x			x		x	x		x	x	x	x	x	x	x		x	x		x			22
Other Instr.	x	x		x			x			x		x		x	x		x		x	x				x								x			x			14

Type B (two corners).

Instrument no.	1	2	3	4	5	6	7	8	9	10	11	12	13	14	15	16	17	18	19	20	21	22	23	24	25	26	27	28	29	30	31	32	33	Summary
Male		x		x		x				x		x	x	x			x	x	x					x	x	x	x	(x)	x	x	x			17
Female																																		
Angel			x		x	x	x		x	x				x						x	x	x	x				x				x			12
None	x		x									x					x						x											4
Alone	x	x			x			x			x		x			x						x	x	x					x					11
Other Instr.		x	x	x		x				x		x			x	x		x	x	x		x	x						x	x		x		16

Type C (no corners, or guitar form).

Instrument no.	1	2	3	4	5	6	7	8	9	10	11	12	13	14	15	16	17	18	19	20	21	Summary
Male					x	x	x		x			x	x					x				7
Female								x														1
Angel	x	x		x			x			x			x		x	x	x		x			10
None		x	x											x								3
Alone					x	x	x		x			x	x									5
Other Instr.	x	x	x	x					x	x			x	x		x	x	x	x			12

D (total shapes not visible).

Instrument no.	1	2	3	4	Summary
Male		x	x	x	3
Female					
Angel	x				1
None					
Alone		x	x	x	3
Other Instr.	x				1

E (oval shape).

Instrument no.	1	Summary
Male	x	1
Female		
Angel		
None		
Alone		
Other Instr.	x	1

Totals for all:					
Male	54				
Female		3			
Angel		26			
None			13		
Alone				41	
Other Instr.					44

This chart indicates the player association in the iconographical examples where liras da braccio appear. Over half of the examples show a male player, the rest show female, angel, or no player. Although it is difficult to determine the gender of angels, most appear to be female. In 41 examples a single lira da braccio player is shown. In 44 examples other instruments are present, such as lute, harp, or wind instruments, but no more than one lira da braccio is ever present in a single example.

LIRA DA BRACCIO INSTRUMENTS IN ICONOGRAPHY: COORDINATE OF SUBJECT AND PLAYER ASSOCIATION.

Mythology

Instrument no.	1	2	3	4	5	6	7	8	9	10	11	12	13	14	15	16	17	18	19	20	21	22	23	24	25	26	27	28	29	30	31	32	33	34	35	36	37	Summary
Type A Male	x		x			x		x		x	x	x	x	x			x		x	x				x		x		x							x	x		17
Type B Male					x						x	x					x	x					x	x			x	x										9
Type C Male				x		x					x																											3
Type D Male		x																																				1
Type E Male	x																																					1

Totals for Mythology: 31

Religious

Instrument no.	Player	1	2	3	4	5	6	7	8	9	10	11	12	13	14	15	16	17	18	19	20	21	22	23	24	25	26	27	28	29	30	31	32	33	34	35	36	37	Male	Female	Angel	None
Type A	Male																							x				x											2			
	Female																																									
	Angel		x		x												x																								3	
	None																																									
Type B	Male		x															x									x				x								4			
	Female																																									
	Angel				x		x	x	x		x	x				x						x	x	x					x				x								12	
	None																		x																							1
Type C	Male																		x																				1			
	Female																																									
	Angel	x	x		x			x			x			x			x	x	x		x																				10	
	None				x																																					1
Type D	Male																																									
	Female																																									
	Angel	x																																							1	
	None																																									

Totals for Religious: 7 | 26 | 2

Secular   (x) = Probable but not counted.

Instrument no.	Player	1	2	3	4	5	6	7	8	9	10	11	12	13	14	15	16	17	18	19	20	21	22	23	24	25	26	27	28	29	30	31	32	33	34	35	36	37	Male	Female	Angel	None
Type A	Male				x					x					x					x				x			x			x				x					7			
	Female						x												x																					2		
	Angel																																									
	None								x															x					x	x	x			x								6
Type B	Male				x					x					x									x						(x)									4			
	Female																																									
	Angel																																									
	None	x	x																						x																	3
Type C	Male						x			x			x																										3			
	Female								x																															1		
	Angel																																									
	None			x												x																										2
Type D	Male			x	x																																		2			
	Female																																									
	Angel																																									
	None																																									

Totals for Secular: 16 | 3 | | 11

Totals for all Types	
Male	54
Female	3
Angel	26
None	13

This chart shows coordinates of subject and player association in the iconographical examples where liras da braccio appear. Mythological subject matter shows only male players. Religious subject matter shows predominantly angel players, who appear to be cherubs or females. Secular subject matter shows mainly male players or none at all.

LIRA DA BRACCIO: DATES OF ICONOGRAPHY AND EXTANT INSTRUMENTS

Total of 107 examples: 97 in iconography and 10 extant instruments.

Type A (four corners, or violin form).

Instrument no.	1	2–16	17	18	19	20	21	22	23–27	28	29	30	31	32–36	37	Summary
End of 15 c.	X															1
1st 3rd 16 c.		X														15
2nd " "				X		X	X									3
3rd " "									X			X	X			7
Begin 17 c.													X	X		6
Unclear				X					X					X		5

Extants	1	2	3	4	5	6	7	8	9	10	Summary
End of 15 c.											
1st 3rd 16 c.				X							1
2nd " "			X								1
3rd " "				X							1
Begin 17 c.											
Unclear	X	X	X			X	X				5

Totals for A: 1 16 4 8 6 | 10

Type B (two corners).

Instrument no.	1	2	3	4–18	19	20–33	28	30	34	Summary
End of 15 c.	X	X	X							3
1st 3rd 16 c.				X		X				25
2nd " "							X	X		2
Unclear					X		X	X		4

Extants	1	2	3	4	5	6	7	8	9	10	Summary
last 3rd 16 c.								X			1
Unclear					X						1

Totals for B: 3 25 2 1 | 5

Type C (no corners, or guitar form).

Instrument no.	1	2	3	4	5–18	13	15	16	Summary
End of 15 c.	X	X	X	X					4
1st 3rd 16 c.					X				14
2nd " "						X			1
Unclear							X	X	2

D (total shapes not visible).

Instrument no.	1	2	3	4	Summary
End of 15 c.	X				1
1st 3rd 16 c.			X		1
Unclear		X	X		2

E (oval shape).

Instrument no.	1	Summary
1st 3rd 16 c.	X	1

Totals for all:

End of 15 c.	9
1st 3rd 16 c.	57
2nd " "	7
3rd " "	9
Begin 17 c.	6
Unclear	19

This chart shows approximate dates of the iconographical examples and extant instruments. Exact dates could not be determined for all iconographical examples, but death dates of the artists, when known, were used to place the examples into approximate thirds of a century. Type A, or violin shapes, span the entire historical time range of the lira da braccio, from the end of the 15th, through the 16th, into the 17th century. All the other types in the iconography are restricted almost entirely to the first third of the 16th century, reflecting the period of highest popularity of the lira da braccio. Dates of most extant insrtuments are either unclear or controversial, but most probably date from the second half of the 16th century.

LIRA DA BRACCIO: TYPE OF ICONOGRAPHY

Total of 97 examples plus two double representations making 99.

Type A (four corners, or violin form).

Instr. no.	1	2	3	4	5	6	7	8	9	10	11	12	13	14	15	16	17	18	19	20	21	22	23	24	25	26	27	28	29	30	31	32	33	34	35	36	37	Summary
Intarsia							x																															1
Woodcut	x		x		x			x		x			x					x			x										x		x					10
Engraving		x					x		x		x	x					x							x			x	x			x							9
Painting				x		x			x							x	x	x		x		x		x				x		x	x		x					12
Drawing																		x	x		x			x											x			5
Watercolor																											x											1
Fresco																																						
Bronze			x																											x								2

Type B (two corners).

Instr. no.	1	2	3	4	5	6	7	8	9	10	11	12	13	14	15	16	17	18	19	20	21	22	23	24	25	26	27	28	29	30	31	32	33	34	Summary
Intarsia			x														x																		2
Woodcut	x	x													x			x	x	x			x	x	x	x				x					11
Engraving				x																															1
Painting				x	x	x		x	x	x	x	x	x			x				x	x	x			x	x	x	x	x		x				18
Drawing													x						x																2
Watercolor																																			
Fresco													x																						1
Bronze																																			

Type C (no corners, or guitar form).

Instr. no.	1	2	3	4	5	6	7	8	9	10	11	12	13	14	15	16	17	18	19	20	21	Summary
Intarsia			x																			1
Woodcut						x		x			x	x		x								5
Engraving				x																		1
Painting	x	x		x			x	x			x			x				x	x			9
Drawing																						
Watercolor																						
Fresco							x						x	x	x							4
Bronze			x																			1

D (total shapes not visible).

Instr. no.	1	2	3	4	Summary
Painting	x	x	x	x	4

E (oval shape).

Instr. no.	1	Summary
Engraving	x	1

Totals for all:

	Total
Intarsia	4
Woodcut	26
Engraving	12
Painting	43
Drawing	7
Watercolor	1
Fresco	5
Bronze	3

This chart indicates the type of iconography in which the lira da braccio examples appear. Most are in the form of paintings, woodcuts, and engravings from northern Italy. They date from the first third of the 16th century, giving evidence that this area was the center of lira da braccio popularity, particularly in the social environment of the courts of Verona, Padua, Mantua, and Venice. Some of the most detailed representations of liras da braccio are to be seen in paintings located in Venice (A-5, B-12), Parma (B-9, see Frontispiece), and Milan (B-5), all dating from about 1505-10. All extant instruments also originate from northern Italy.

LIRA DA BRACCIO BOWS IN ICONOGRAPHY

With instruments of type A. Total of 36 examples.

Bow length	1	2	3	4	5	6	7	8	9	10	11	12	13	14	15	16	17	18	19	20	21	22	23	24	25	26	27	28	29	30	31	32	33	34	35	36	37	Totals
Long	x[a]			x											x									x														4
Medium		x			x	x			x		x	x					x	x	x	x							x				x		x					13
Short	x[b]		x					x		x			x										x	x	x		x	x	x	x		x	x		x	x	x	17
Unclear							x									x																						2

Bow shape	1	2	3	4	5	6	7	8	9	10	11	12	13	14	15	16	17	18	19	20	21	22	23	24	25	26	27	28	29	30	31	32	33	34	35	36	37	Totals
High arch					x			x		x				x			x							x	x				x						x			10
Medium arch	x[b]	x		x		x			x		x	x				x				x					x		x										x	13
Low arch														x					x		x	x	x					x			x		x	x				9
Straight			x				x																									x						3
Unclear																	x																					1

On strings at:	1	2	3	4	5	6	7	8	9	10	11	12	13	14	15	16	17	18	19	20	21	22	23	24	25	26	27	28	29	30	31	32	33	34	35	36	37	Totals
Lower 3rd																																				x		1
Mid 3rd		x		x						x		x			x			x						x			x				x		x					10
Upper 3rd	x[b]							x			x																											3
Not on strings	x[a]		x		x	x	x		x				x	x		x	x		x	x	x	x	x		x		x	x	x		x	x	x		x			22

Bridge distance	1	2	3	4	5	6	7	8	9	10	11	12	13	14	15	16	17	18	19	20	21	22	23	24	25	26	27	28	29	30	31	32	33	34	35	36	37	Totals
Near	x[b]																								x													2
Normal																																						
Far					x						x		x																				x		x	x		6
No bridge		x		x				x				x		x															x									5

Size of frog	1	2	3	4	5	6	7	8	9	10	11	12	13	14	15	16	17	18	19	20	21	22	23	24	25	26	27	28	29	30	31	32	33	34	35	36	37	Totals
Large	x[b]		x		x						x																x											5
Medium						x	x		x		x		x				x			x			x	x				x	x	x	x		x		x			15
Small																						x			x													2
None		(x)		x				x						x													x											(1) 4
Unclear	x[a]											x					x	x		x							x					x		x				8

Hand on bow	1	2	3	4	5	6	7	8	9	10	11	12	13	14	15	16	17	18	19	20	21	22	23	24	25	26	27	28	29	30	31	32	33	34	35	36	37	Totals
Near or at end		x		x							x	x	x				x	x						x	x	x	x								x			13
Away from end	x[b]		x		x	x		x						x	x				x	x	x							x			x		x			x		14
Fingers on hair	x[b]								(x)									(x)																			x	(2) 2
Unclear																																						

| No bow shown | | x | | | | | | | | | | | | | | | | | | | | | | | | | | x | | | | | | | | | | 2 |

This chart indicates bow characteristics in the iconography shown with the type A lira da braccio. Iconographical examples of this type represent the longest time span in the history of the lira da braccio and consequently show a large variety of bow characteristics without revealing any particular trends. About two-thirds of the examples show the bows held away from the strings.

LIRA DA BRACCIO BOWS IN ICONOGRAPHY

With instruments of type B. Total of 30 examples.

Bow length	1	2	3	4	5	6	7	8	9	10	11	12	13	14	15	16	17	18	19	20	21	22	23	24	25	26	27	28	29	30	31	32	33	34		Totals
Long					x	x	x	x					x	x		x	x					x	x			x	x									12
Medium	x																			x	x			x							x					5
Short			x		x			x		x	x			x			x												x	x	x		x			11
Unclear																			x							x										2
Bow shape	1	2	3	4	5	6	7	8	9	10	11	12	13	14	15	16	17	18	19	20	21	22	23	24	25	26	27	28	29	30	31	32	33	34		
High arch								x										x																		2
Medium arch		x		x			x	x			x	(x)	x	x	x	x				x	x			x	x	x			x	x	x	x	x			(1) 19
Low arch				x	x																			x												3
Straight	x																x	x																		3
Unclear																							x				x									2
On strings at:	1	2	3	4	5	6	7	8	9	10	11	12	13	14	15	16	17	18	19	20	21	22	23	24	25	26	27	28	29	30	31	32	33	34		
Lower 3rd											x																x	x								3
Mid 3rd				x		x	x	x						x								x														6
Upper 3rd		x			x											x		x		x			x	x		x	x	x			x					11
Not on strings	x							x			x			x		x	x	x														x	x			9
Bridge distance	1	2	3	4	5	6	7	8	9	10	11	12	13	14	15	16	17	18	19	20	21	22	23	24	25	26	27	28	29	30	31	32	33	34		
Near						x															x															2
Normal					x			(x)					x	x									x	x												(1) 5
Far		x		x				(x)			x					x				x							x		x	x	x					(1) 9
No bridge																								(x)	(x)											(2)
Size of frog	1	2	3	4	5	6	7	8	9	10	11	12	13	14	15	16	17	18	19	20	21	22	23	24	25	26	27	28	29	30	31	32	33	34		
Large								x										x						x								x				4
Medium									x						x	x		x		x	x		x				x				x					9
Small	x				x	x								x												x										5
None		x																							x											2
Unclear				x			x					x	x	x					x				x					x	x							9
Hand on bow	1	2	3	4	5	6	7	8	9	10	11	12	13	14	15	16	17	18	19	20	21	22	23	24	25	26	27	28	29	30	31	32	33	34		
Near or at end							x						x	x													x				x	x				6
Away from end		x		x	x	x			x	x		x	x				x				x	x	x	x		x	x			x						16
Fingers on hair				(x)																x				x	x											(1) 3
Unclear																												x								1
No bow shown			x						x														x										x			4

This chart indicates bow characteristics in the iconography shown with the type B lira da braccio. Inasmuch as this type is essentially restricted to the first third of the 16th century, some bow characteristics may indicate a few trends which are not necessarily related to this shape. Even though long bows are observed as often as short ones, long bows appear more frequently in this time span than later. Seven of the twelve long bows are held away from the lower end, that is, with the hand placed higher on the stick, which aids in balancing long bows.

LIRA DA BRACCIO BOWS IN ICONOGRAPHY

With instruments of type C. Total of 18 examples.

Bow length	1	2	3	4	5	6	7	8	9	10	11	12	13	14	15	16	17	18	19	20	21	Totals
Long				x		x								x								3
Medium					x						x	x	x		x			x		x	x	8
Short	x	x				x	x	x								x			x			7
Unclear																						

Bow shape	1	2	3	4	5	6	7	8	9	10	11	12	13	14	15	16	17	18	19	20	21	Totals
High arch		x		x		x							x			x						5
Medium arch				x		x					x	x		x	x			x		x	x	9
Low arch	x							x	x									x				4
Straight																						
Unclear																						

On strings at:	1	2	3	4	5	6	7	8	9	10	11	12	13	14	15	16	17	18	19	20	21	Totals
Lower 3rd		x																				1
Mid 3rd					x		x	x			x								x			5
Upper 3rd	x			x		x				x			x	x	x		x	x		x		10
Not on strings									x							x						2

Bridge distance	1	2	3	4	5	6	7	8	9	10	11	12	13	14	15	16	17	18	19	20	21	Totals
Near																						
Normal				x	x		x							x				x	x			6
Far	x	x						x			x	x		x				x				7
No bridge						x			x													2

Size of frog	1	2	3	4	5	6	7	8	9	10	11	12	13	14	15	16	17	18	19	20	21	Totals
Large																	x		x			2
Medium	x							x	x													3
Small		x				x																2
None				x											x	x						3
Unclear					x		x				x	x	x	x				x	x			8

Hand on bow	1	2	3	4	5	6	7	8	9	10	11	12	13	14	15	16	17	18	19	20	21	Totals
Near or at end	x			x	x	x	x	x			x		x	x	x			x	x	x	x	14
Away from end		x																				1
Fingers on hair	x	x																				2
Unclear												x										1

No bow shown	1	2	3	4	5	6	7	8	9	10	11	12	13	14	15	16	17	18	19	20	21	Totals
No bow shown		x	x													x						3

This chart indicates bow characteristics in the iconography shown with the type C lira da braccio. With even fewer examples of bows shown with this type, any trends which emerge may have little significance. Some correlation can be observed here between bow length and arch--less arch with a shorter bow--but this can hardly be considered a trend since some examples reveal the opposite. Hand positions are noticably at or near the lower end of the bows, relating to the fact that fewer long bows are seen in these examples. Short bows would not require a higher hand position on the stick (see previous chart).

LIRA DA BRACCIO BOWS IN ICONOGRAPHY
Total of 87 examples.

With instruments of: type D	1	2	3	4	Totals	type E. 1	Totals
Bow length							
Long						x	1
Medium							
Short							
Unclear	x		x		2		
Bow shape							
High arch						x	1
Medium arch	x				1		
Low arch							
Straight			(x)		(1)		
Unclear							
On strings at:							
Lower 3rd							
Mid 3rd	(x)				(1)		
Upper 3rd							
Not on strings			x		1	x	1
Bridge distance							
Near							
Normal							
Far							
No bridge							
Size of frog							
Large							
Medium							
Small							
None						x	1
Unclear							
Hand on bow							
Near or at end						x	1
Away from end							
Fingers on hair							
Unclear							
No bow shown		x		x	2		

	A 36	B 30	C 18	D 2	E 1	Totals
Bow length						
Long	4	12	3		1	20
Medium	13	5	8			26
Short	17	11	7			35
Unclear	2	2		2		6
Bow shape						
High arch	10	2	5		1	18
Medium arch	13	(1) 19	9	1		(1) 42
Low arch	9	3	4			16
Straight	3	3		(1)		(1) 6
Unclear	1	2				3
On strings at:						
Lower 3rd	1	3	1			5
Mid 3rd	10	6	5	(1)		(1) 21
Upper 3rd	3	11	10			24
Not on strings	22	9	2	1	1	35
Bridge distance						
Near	2	2				4
Normal		(1) 5	6			11
Far	6	(1) 9	7			(1) 22
No bridge	5	(2)	2			(2) 7
Size of frog						
Large	5	4	2			11
Medium	15	9	3			27
Small	2	5	2			9
None	(1) 4	2	3		1	10
Unclear	8	9	8			25
Hand on bow						
Near or at end	13	6	14		1	34
Away from end	14	16	1			31
Fingers on hair	(2) 2	(1) 3	2			(3) 7
Unclear		1		1		2
No bow shown	2	4	3	2		11

This chart indicates bow characteristics in the iconography shown with lira da braccio instruments of type D and type E, with a summary of totals for all types. Some aspects about bow characteristics are revealed in observing the totals for all the iconographicl examples. Even though the use of long bows for lira da braccio instruments is mentioned in some sources (Ganassi, Rognoni) the predominance of such bows is not borne out by the examples. These show mainly medium to short bows. Most bows show medium shaped arches of the stick and medium size frogs, although in many examples this is difficult to judge. Bow placements on the strings tend to be in the middle or upper ends of the bows, far from the bridges. Hand positions on bows are fairly equally divided between place-ments at or near the bow ends, and placements higher on the sticks whereby these are related to the length of bows in many examples (see type B and type C).

LIRA DA BRACCIO BOWS IN ICONOGRAPHY: BOW LENGTHS
Total of 81 clear examples.

With instruments of type A.

Bow length	1	2	3	4	5	6	7	8	9	10	11	12	13	14	15	16	17	18	19	20	21	22	23	24	25	26	27	28	29	30	31	32	33	34	35	36	37	Totals
Long	x[a]			x										x												x												4
Medium		x				x	x			x		x	x				x	x	x	x	x									x			x					13
Short	x[b]			x				x		x					x								x	x	x			x	x	x	x		x	x	x	x	x	17
Unclear								x									x																					2

With instruments of type B.

Bow length	1	2	3	4	5	6	7	8	9	10	11	12	13	14	15	16	17	18	19	20	21	22	23	24	25	26	27	28	29	30	31	32	33	34	Totals
Long					x	x	x	x					x	x		x	x					x	x			x	x								12
Medium	x																		x	x				x							x				5
Short		x		x					x		x	x			x			x										x	x	x		x			11
Unclear																				x								x							2

With instruments of type C.

Bow length	1	2	3	4	5	6	7	8	9	10	11	12	13	14	15	16	17	18	19	20	21	Totals
Long				x		x							x									3
Medium					x				x	x	x		x			x		x	x			8
Short	x	x					x	x	x					x			x					7
Unclear																						

With instruments of type D.

Bow length	1	2	3	4	Totals
Long					
Medium					
Short					
Unclear	x		x		2

With type E instrument.

Bow length	1	Totals
Long	x	1
Medium		
Short		
Unclear		

Bow length	Totals
Long	20
Medium	26
Short	35
Unclear	6

This chart gives details of bow lengths shown with all types of lira da braccio in the iconographical examples. Even though the use of long bows is mentioned in some sources (Ganassi, Rognoni), the predominance of such bows is not borne out by the examples, which show mainly medium to short bows. The examples showing long bows date almost entirely from the first third of the 16th century, the high point in lira da braccio history. They are to be seen mainly in type B instruments.

LIRA DA BRACCIO BOWS IN ICONOGRAPHY: BOW SHAPES
Total of 82 clear examples.

(x) = Probable but not counted.

With instruments of type A.

Bow shape	1	2	3	4	5	6	7	8	9	10	11	12	13	14	15	16	17	18	19	20	21	22	23	24	25	26	27	28	29	30	31	32	33	34	35	36	37	Totals
High arch					x			x		x			x				x		x							x	x			x				x				10
Medium "	x	x			x		x			x		x	x				x			x						x		x						x			x	13
Low arch														x						x			x	x	x				x			x	x	x				9
Straight			x				x																										x					3
Unclear																		x																				1

With instruments of type B.

Bow shape	1	2	3	4	5	6	7	8	9	10	11	12	13	14	15	16	17	18	19	20	21	22	23	24	25	26	27	28	29	30	31	32	33	34	Totals
High arch						x												x																	2
Medium "		x		x			x	x			x	(x)	x	x	x	x			x	x			x	x	x		x	x	x	x	x				19
Low arch				x	x																	x													3
Straight	x																x	x																	3
Unclear																							x					x							2

With instruments of type C.

Bow shape	1	2	3	4	5	6	7	8	9	10	11	12	13	14	15	16	17	18	19	20	21	Totals
High arch		x			x		x					x			x							5
Medium "					x		x			x	x		x	x			x		x	x		9
Low arch	x							x	x								x					4
Straight																						
Unclear																						

With instruments of type D.

Bow shape	1	2	3	4	Totals
High arch					
Medium "	x				1
Low arch					
Straight		(x)			
Unclear					

With type E instrument.

Bow shape	1	Totals
High arch	x	1
Medium "		
Low arch		
Straight		
Unclear		

Bow shape	Totals
High arch	18
Medium "	42
Low arch	16
Straight	6
Unclear	3

This chart gives details of bow shapes shown with all types of lira da braccio in the iconographical examples. Although it is often difficult to determine bow shapes because of variations in perspective, an attempt has been made at classification. Even though a great variety of shapes and lengths are seen in combination throughout the range of examples, most appear to have bows with medium-size arches often correlated to medium bow lengths. Some bows have straight sticks, and a few even show characteristics of a much later period (B-1, D-3).

LIRA DA BRACCIO BOWS IN ICONOGRAPHY: BOW POSITION ON STRINGS
Total of 50 examples.

With instruments of type A.   (x) = Probable but not counted.

On strings at	1	2	3	4	5	6	7	8	9	10	11	12	13	14	15	16	17	18	19	20	21	22	23	24	25	26	27	28	29	30	31	32	33	34	35	36	37	Totals
Lower 3rd																																				x		1
Mid 3rd		x		x						x	x			x		x								x			x				x	x						10
Upper 3rd	xb					x			x																													3
Off strings	xa		x		x	x	x		x			x	x		x	x			x	x	x	x	x		x		x	x		x	x	x		x				22

With instruments of type B.

On strings at	1	2	3	4	5	6	7	8	9	10	11	12	13	14	15	16	17	18	19	20	21	22	23	24	25	26	27	28	29	30	31	32	33	34	Totals
Lower 3rd												x																	x	x					3
Mid 3rd				x		x	x	x					x							x															6
Upper 3rd		x		x										x		x			x			x	x		x	x	x				x				11
Off strings	x						x			x				x		x	x	x													x	x			9

With instruments of type C.

On strings at	1	2	3	4	5	6	7	8	9	10	11	12	13	14	15	16	17	18	19	20	21	Totals
Lower 3rd		x																				1
Mid 3rd					x		x	x			x							x				5
Upper 3rd	x			x		x			x	x	x			x	x		x					10
Off strings							x						x									2

With instruments of type D.

On strings at	1	2	3	4	Totals
Lower 3rd					
Mid 3rd	(x)				
Upper 3rd					
Off strings			x		1

With type E instrument.

On strings at	1	Totals
Lower 3rd		
Mid 3rd		
Upper 3rd		
Off strings	x	1

On strings at	
Lower 3rd	5
Mid 3rd	21
Upper 3rd	24
Off strings	35

This chart gives details of bow positions on the strings of all types of lira da braccio in the iconographical examples. Of the 50 examples which show bow placement on the strings, almost all are in the mid- to upper third of the bow. This, in combination with the fact that short bows are often shown on the strings far from the bridges, leads to the conclusion that chords were lightly stroked rather than sustained. The physics of such a relationship between bow and string hardly permits long, sustained chords. On the other hand, this situation may have led to the comments of Ganassi and Rognoni that long bows should be used with the lira (see above "Some Early Citations," pp. 7, 8).

LIRA DA BRACCIO BOWS IN ICONOGRAPHY: BOW POSITION RELATIVE TO BRIDGE
Total of 37 clear examples.

With instruments of type A.   (x) = Probable but not counted.

From bridge	1	2	3	4	5	6	7	8	9	10	11	12	13	14	15	16	17	18	19	20	21	22	23	24	25	26	27	28	29	30	31	32	33	34	35	36	37	Totals
Near	x b																										x											2
Normal																																						
Far				x							x		x																				x		x	x		6
No bridge		x			x			x			x															x												5

With instruments of type B.

From bridge	1	2	3	4	5	6	7	8	9	10	11	12	13	14	15	16	17	18	19	20	21	22	23	24	25	26	27	28	29	30	31	32	33	34	Totals
Near						x															x														2
Normal				x			(x)							x	x									x	x										5
Far		x		x			(x)				x						x				x								x	x	x	x			9
No bridge																									(x)	(x)									

With instruments of type C.

From bridge	1	2	3	4	5	6	7	8	9	10	11	12	13	14	15	16	17	18	19	20	21	Totals
Near																						
Normal					x	x		x						x				x	x			6
Far	x	x							x		x	x	x		x			x				7
No bridge						x			x													2

With instruments of type D.

From bridge	1	2	3	4	Totals
Near					
Normal					
Far					
No bridge					

With type E instrument.

From bridge	1	Totals
Near		
Normal		
Far		
No bridge		

From bridge		
Near	4	
Normal	11	
Far	22	
No bridge		7

This chart gives details of bow positions relative to bridges on all types of lira da braccio in the iconographical examples. Of the examples which show bows on the strings, 37 reveal their positions relative to bridges. These placements are not always easy to determine because of perspective angles. About two-thirds of the examples show bow positions far from bridges, and about one-third show what can be considered normal playing positions relative to string lengths. In seven examples, no bridges are visible. The fact that short bows are often shown on the strings far from the bridges leads to the conclusion that chords were lightly stroked rather than sustained. The physics of such a relationship between bow and string hardly permits long, sustained chords. This situation may have led to the comments of Ganassi and Rognoni that long bows should be used with the lira in order to sustain chords (see above "Some Early Citations," pp. 7, 8).

LIRA DA BRACCIO BOWS IN ICONOGRAPHY: FROG SIZE
Total of 46 clear examples.

With instruments of type A. (x) = Probable but not counted.

Size of frog	1	2	3	4	5	6	7	8	9	10	11	12	13	14	15	16	17	18	19	20	21	22	23	24	25	26	27	28	29	30	31	32	33	34	35	36	37	Totals
Large	x^b			x		x					x																	x										5
Medium						x	x		x		x		x			x			x			x	x						x	x	x	x		x		x		15
Small																								x			x											2
None		(x)		x			x							x												x												4
Unclear	x^a												x					x	x		x								x				x		x			8

With instruments of type B.

Size of frog	1	2	3	4	5	6	7	8	9	10	11	12	13	14	15	16	17	18	19	20	21	22	23	24	25	26	27	28	29	30	31	32	33	34				Totals
Large								x									x							x							x							4
Medium							x						x	x		x			x	x		x				x				x								9
Small	x				x	x								x											x													5
None		x																							x													2
Unclear			x			x				x	x	x							x			x						x	x									9

With instruments of type C.

Size of frog	1	2	3	4	5	6	7	8	9	10	11	12	13	14	15	16	17	18	19	20	21				Totals
Large																x			x						2
Medium	x					x	x																		3
Small		x			x																				2
None				x									x	x											3
Unclear				x		x				x	x	x	x				x	x							8

With instruments of type D.

Size of frog	1	2	3	4				Totals
Large								
Medium								
Small								
None								
Unclear								

With type E instrument.

Size of frog	1				Totals
Large					
Medium					
Small					
None	x				1
Unclear					

Size of frog					
Large	11				
Medium		27			
Small			9		
None				10	
Unclear					25

This chart gives details of frog sizes on bows shown in the iconographical examples of all types of lira da braccio. Of the 46 examples, over half show a medium-size frog. Almost all examples showing very large frogs or no frogs occur between the end of the 15th century and the first third of the 16th. Some small frogs appear to be carved as part of the stick itself (B-27, C-7).

LIRA DA BRACCIO BOWS IN ICONOGRAPHY: HAND POSITION
Total of 65 clear examples.

With instruments of type A. (x) = Probable but not counted.

Hand position	1	2	3	4	5	6	7	8	9	10	11	12	13	14	15	16	17	18	19	20	21	22	23	24	25	26	27	28	29	30	31	32	33	34	35	36	37	Totals
Near or at end		x		x							x	x	x				x	x										x	x	x	x					x		13
Away from end	x a				x		x	x		x					x	x				x	x	x										x		x		x		14
Fingers on hair	x b									(x)									(x)																	x		2
Unclear																																						0

With instruments of type B.

Hand position	1	2	3	4	5	6	7	8	9	10	11	12	13	14	15	16	17	18	19	20	21	22	23	24	25	26	27	28	29	30	31	32	33	34	Totals
Near or at end							x						x	x													x				x	x			6
Away from end		x		x	x	x			x	x			x	x				x			x	x	x	x			x	x			x				16
Fingers on hair				(x)																	x						x	x							3
Unclear																														x					1

With instruments of type C.

Hand position	1	2	3	4	5	6	7	8	9	10	11	12	13	14	15	16	17	18	19	20	21	Totals
Near or at end	x				x	x	x	x	x		x		x	x	x			x	x	x	x	14
Away from end		x																				1
Fingers on hair	x	x																				2
Unclear												x										1

With instruments of type D.

Hand position	1	2	3	4			
Near or at end							
Away from end							
Fingers on hair							
Unclear							

With type E instrument.

Hand position	1			
Near or at end	x			1
Away from end				
Fingers on hair				
Unclear				

Hand position	Totals
Near or at end	34
Away from end	31
Fingers on hair	7
Unclear	2

This chart gives details of hand positions on bows shown in the iconographical examples of all types of lira da braccio. Of the 65 examples where hand positions on bows are clear, a fairly equal division can be observed between hand placements near or at the lower ends of bows and placements away from the ends, that is, higher on the sticks. In examples dating from the first third of the 16th century where most long bows are seen, there is a tendency toward hands positioned away from the ends of the bows, a balancing aid in holding long bows. It can be seen that some fingers touch the hair of the bow in seven examples.

Lira da braccio by Giovanni d'Andrea
(Kunsthistorisches Museum, Vienna, Schlosser cat. no. 94)

Lira da braccio by Giovanni d'Andrea
(Kunsthistorisches Museum, Vienna, Schlosser cat. no. 94)

5
Chords and Fingering Charts

These charts indicate how open strings are tuned and show chord fingerings for first, second and third positions. Major, minor, seventh, diminished, and augmented chords plus the commonly used four-three progressions are shown for all twelve key signatures. The numbers refer to open strings and fingerings as they would occur for producing notes with no sharps or flats, as in a C major scale (see fingering chart on p. 85). Additional signs indicate the following:

´ = sharp, ´´ = double sharp, ` = flat, `` = double flat, or their enharmonic equivalents, thus showing raised or lowered fingers from their "accidental free" positions on the string.

t = thumb, or thumb nail against an off-the-fingerboard string.

* = most practical or easiest way to manage chord.

(*) = next most practical or manageable chord.

( ) = additional possibility, or *ad libitum.*

The choice of using the top string d" lira da braccio tuning was made because of the number of interesting chord possibilities offered beyond those with the normal top string e" violin tuning. Decisions as to which chords are more or less practical or easy to manage are of course personal, but they also depend on such matters as string separation, curvature of the bridge, and the hand itself. Certainly not all chord possibilities for the three positions have been exhausted, but more than enough are given for practical application. Because of lack of evidence, it is impossible to know how extensively chords in higher positions were actually used. Their inclusion on these charts is perhaps more academic than practical. The only chords given are those where the root pitch and at least two other pitches are present, these pitches sometimes being only octave doublings. In an accompanying situation, where the root pitch occurs elsewhere, chords from another key can be useful. For example, in a C seventh chord where the root tone is in another part, an E diminished chord can be used in the lira da braccio accompaniment to complete the harmony.

The chords on the following charts are dependent on equidistant string placement on the fingerboard and bridge. They are also dependent on a well-adjusted small curvature of the bridge and tension of the bow. There is some evidence in the iconography of placing the two lowest fingerboard strings close together, that is g-g' (strings 4 and 5), as well as Marini's comment at the beginning of his *Capriccio* (see below, Appendix), and the fact that some chords in the Pesaro Ms. involve stopping three strings with a single finger position. This would of course alter the chord possibilities involving those strings, inasmuch as they could not be fingered separately if they are very close, but this aspect has been disregarded here since most evidence points to equidistant string separation.

As might be expected the greatest variety of chord possibilities occur in the keys of G and D, but also in the key of E because of the use of the d-d' open strings in seventh chords. (There are 45 different ways shown for voicing and fingering this chord!) The number of chord possibilities in all keys is quite surprising.

Experience playing the lira da braccio shows that using all stopped strings for chords is sometimes easier than using a mixture of stopped and open strings, especially for chords executed on inner strings. The strings on the fingerboard are so close together that it is often difficult not to touch the open string of a chord, and sometimes the open string is in a slightly different playing position for the bow. This is evident in the choice of fingerings used in the musical examples. Holding the bow in such a way that the tension can be altered with the fingers, a technique requiring some practice, is useful in separating out single strings when required. This technique is mentioned by Ganassi when he talks about using the viol in a similar manner as the lira da braccio (see above, p. 7).

Lira da braccio: C Chords with Fingering Chart

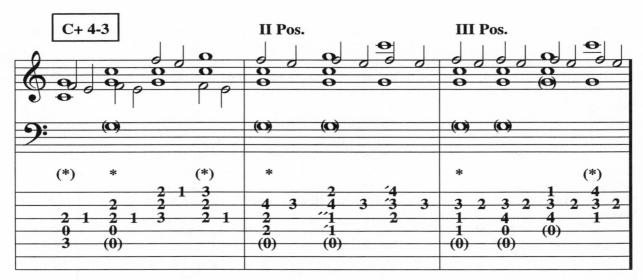

59

Lira da braccio: D♭ (C♯) Chords with Fingering Chart

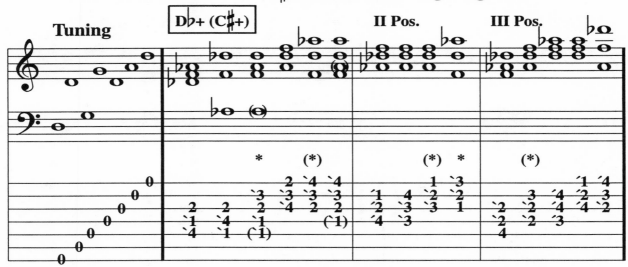

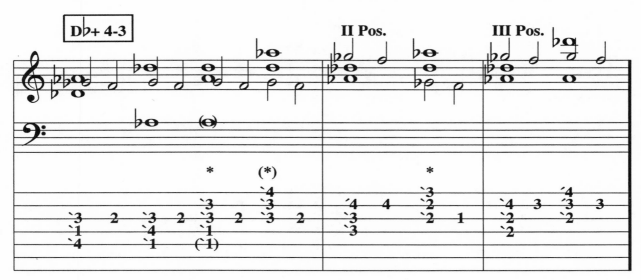

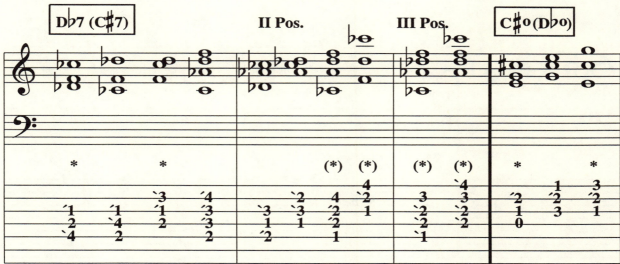

Lira da braccio: D Chords with Fingering Chart

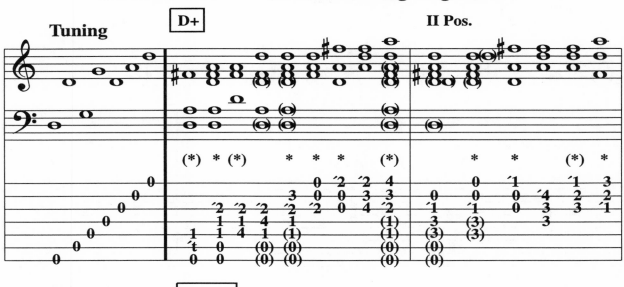

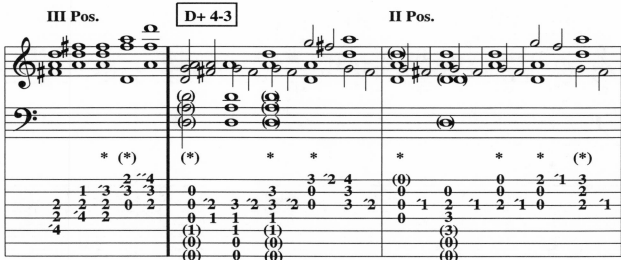

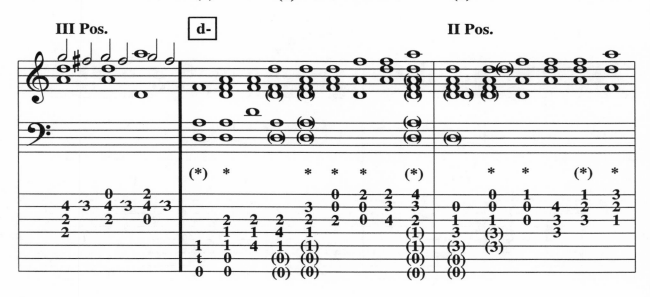

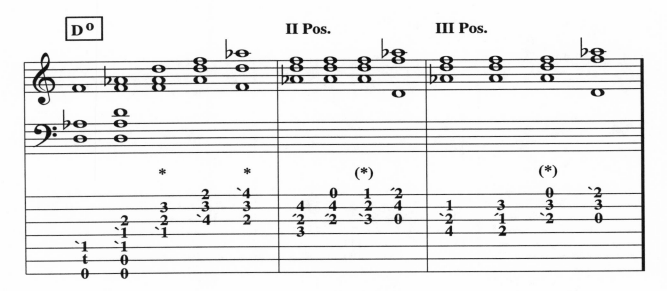

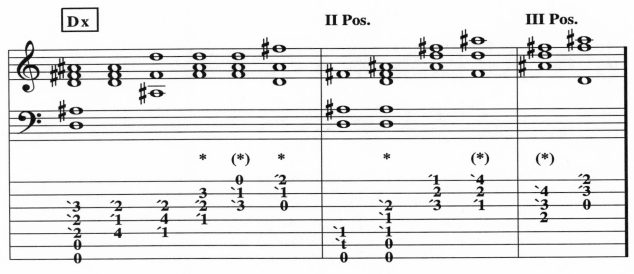

64

Lira da braccio: E♭ Chords with Fingering Chart

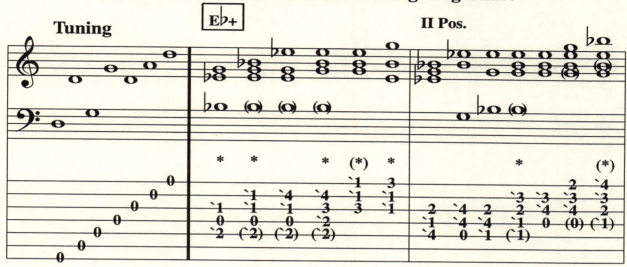

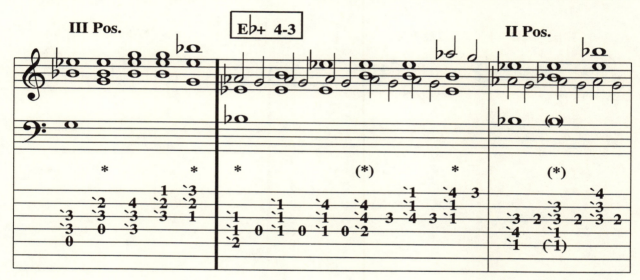

Lira da braccio: E Chords with Fingering Chart

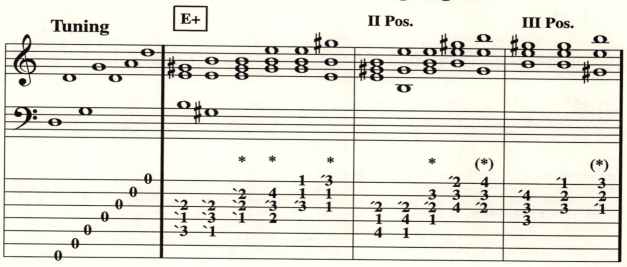

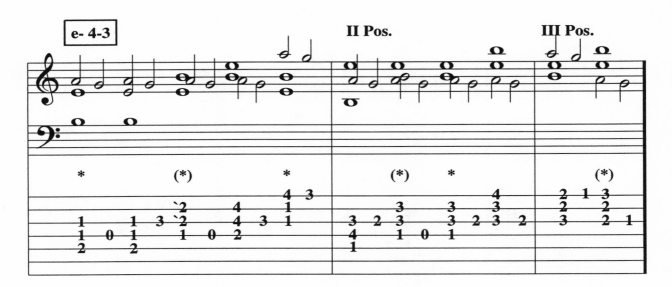

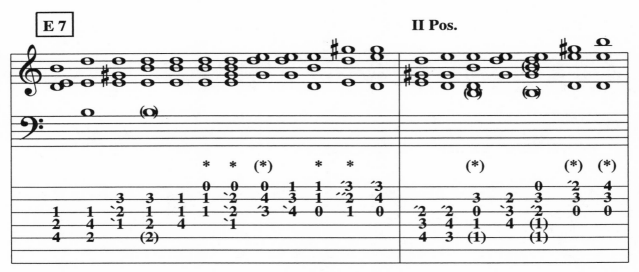

III Pos.   With basso grave and basso acuto strings

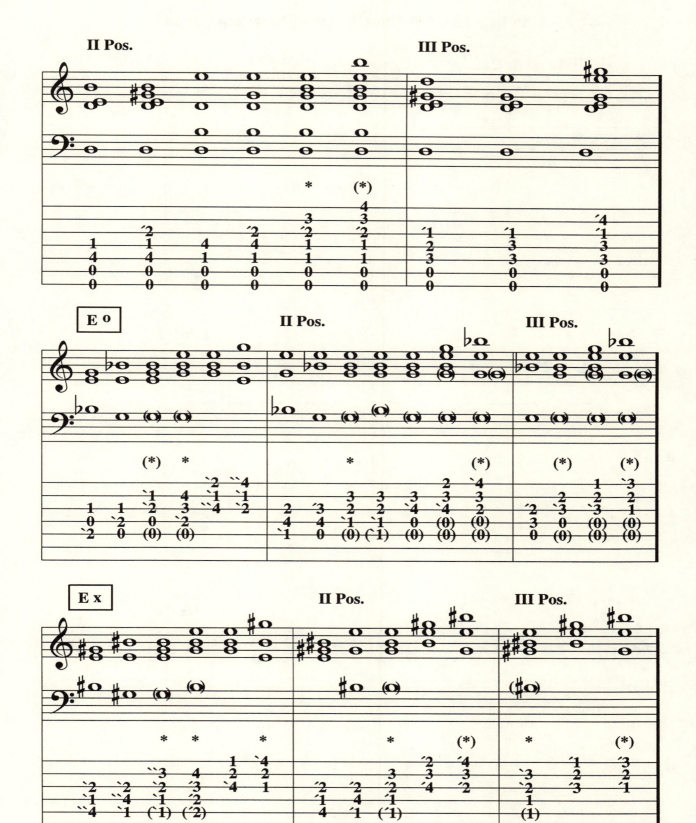

Lira da braccio: F Chords with Fingering Chart

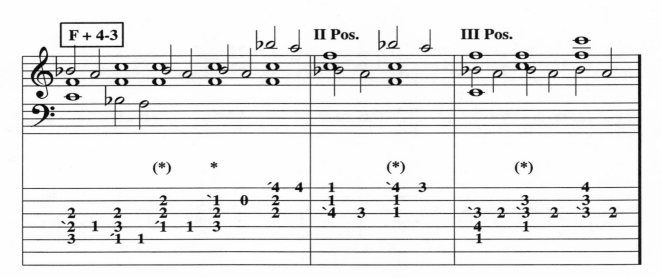

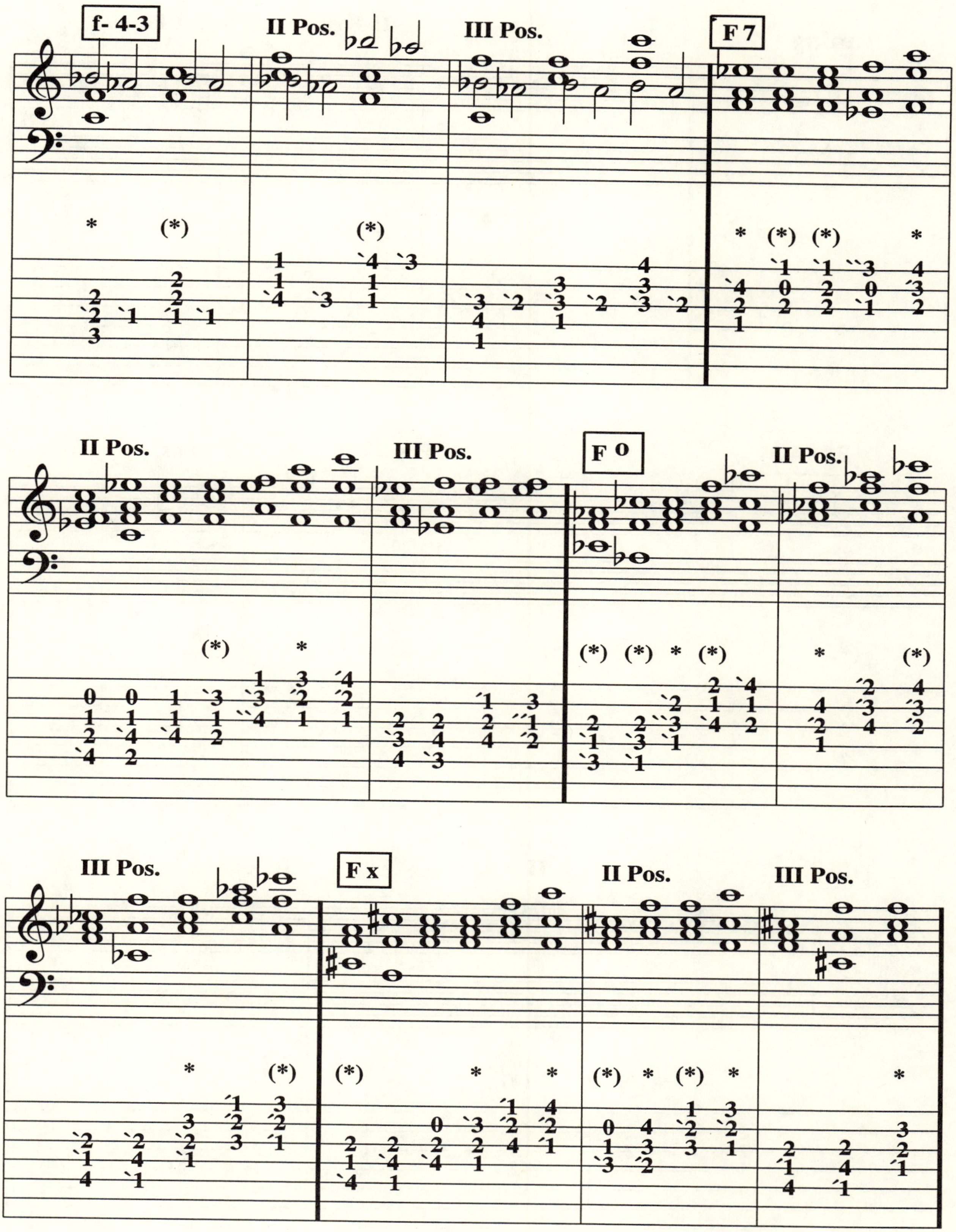
f- 4-3
II Pos.
III Pos.
F 7
II Pos.
III Pos.
F o
II Pos.
III Pos.
F x
II Pos.
III Pos.

Lira da braccio: F♯ (G♭) Chords with Fingering Chart

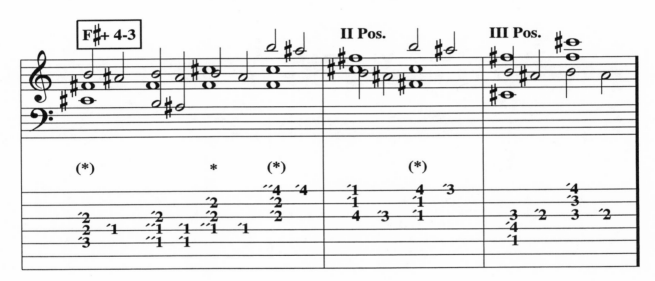

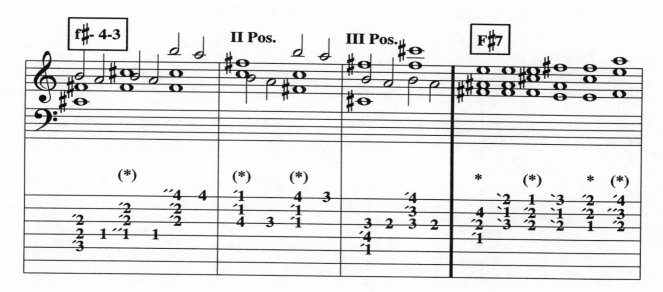

Lira da braccio: G Chords with Fingering Chart

74

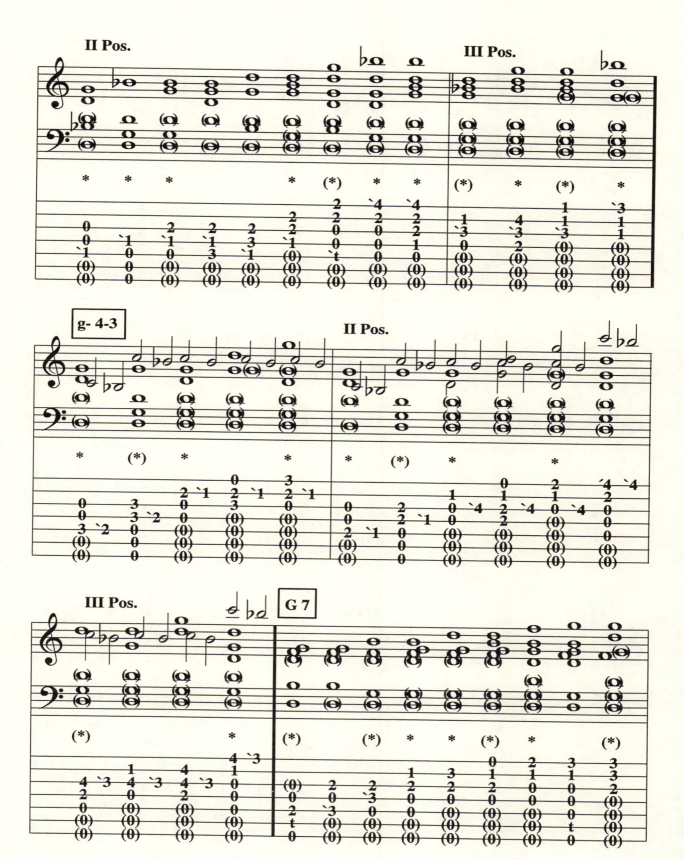

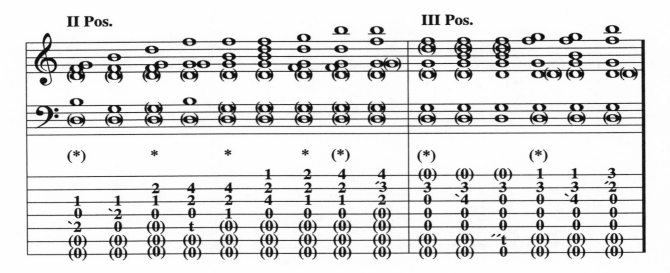

Lira da braccio: A♭ (G♯) Chords with Fingering Chart

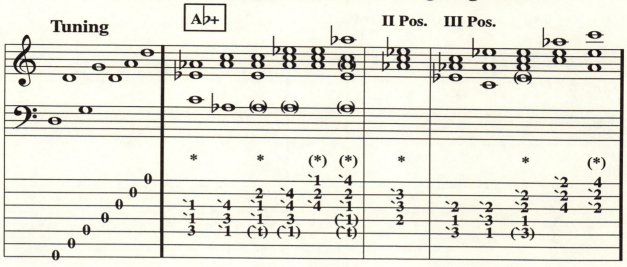

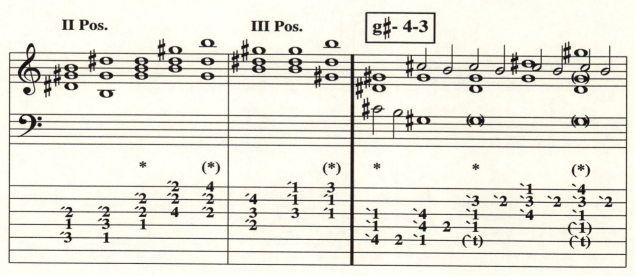

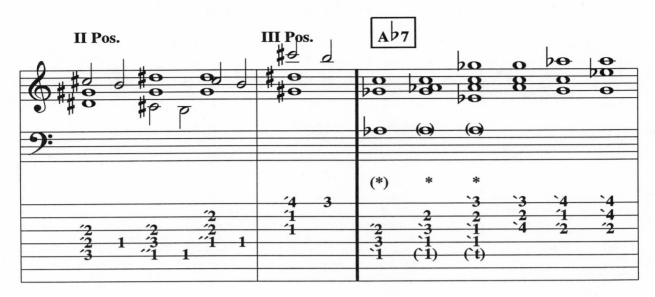

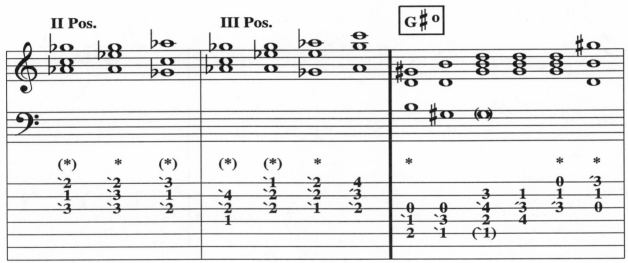

Lira da braccio: A Chords with Fingering Chart

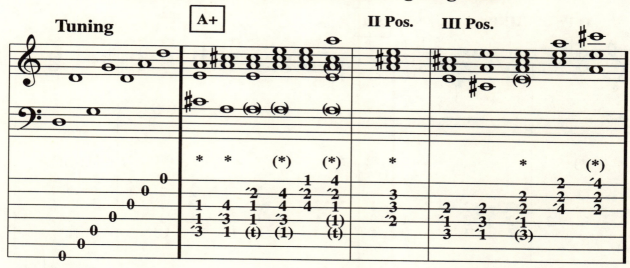

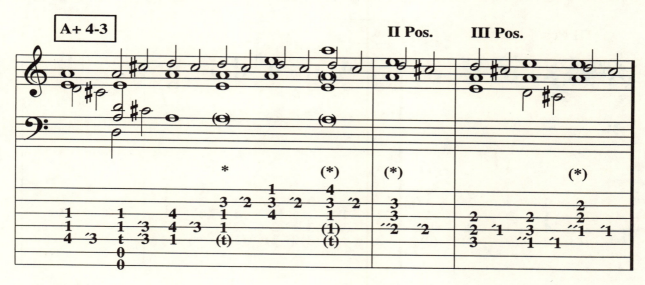

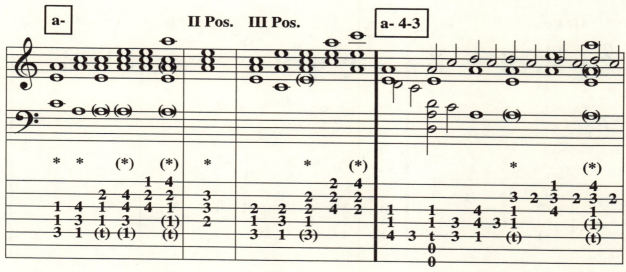

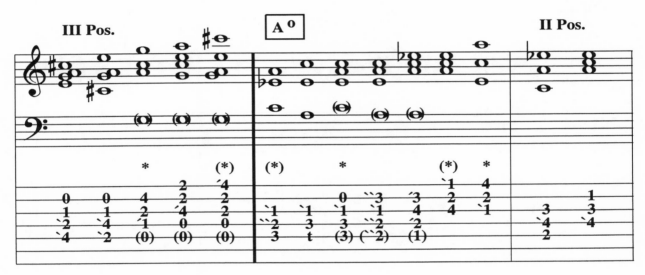

80

Lira da braccio: B♭ Chords with Fingering Chart

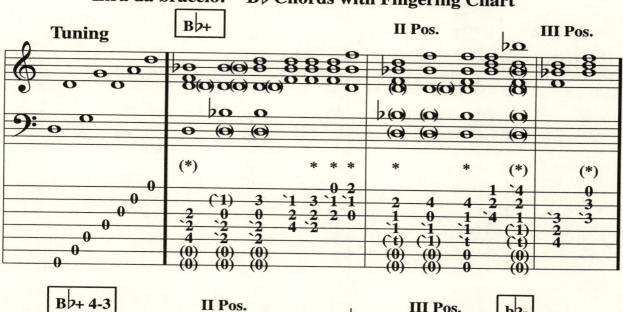

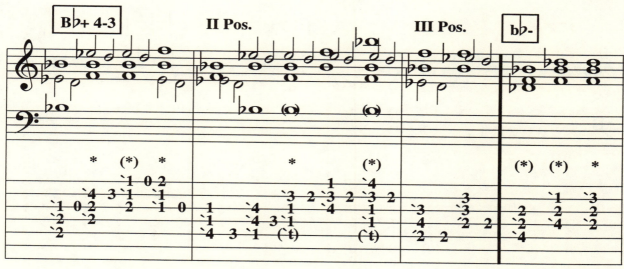

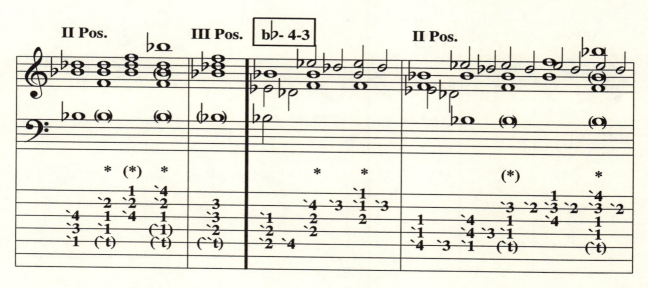

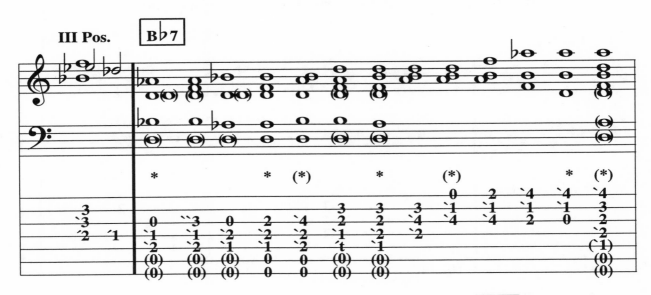

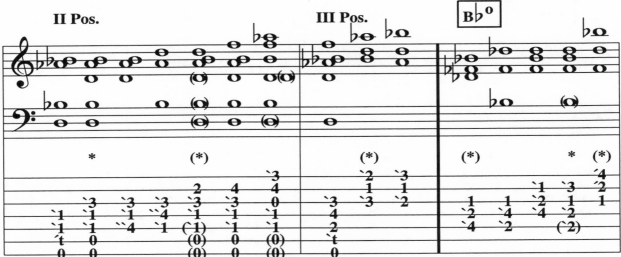

Lira da braccio: B Chords with Fingering Chart

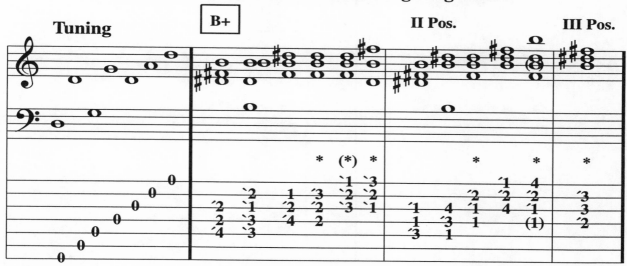

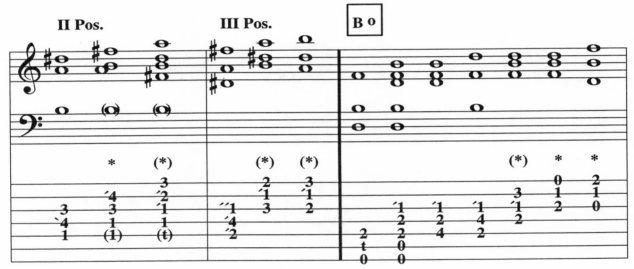

84

6
Selected Repertoire

In light of Mersenne's statement (*peut jouer toutes sortes de pièces de Musique dessus,* see above, p. 8), various types of musical examples have been selected. Those examples using a tuning d-d'/g-g'-d'-a'-d" include three arrangements of *frottole* taken from Petrucci publications, an arrangement of the madrigal *O felici occhi miei* by Arcadelt, accompaniments for the recitatives from *Il Sacrificio* with music by Alfonso della Viola, and the examples from the Pesaro Ms. (see Appendix for the original tablature). The arrangement and accompaniments for *Ayme sospiri* (based on a three-part vocal piece from the Escorial Ms. [see Appendix] which appears in a Petrucci volume with ornamentation) uses an alto tuning G-g/c-c'-g-d'-g'. The arrangement for lira da braccio of the *Capriccio* by Biagio Marini uses the tuning d-d'/g-'-d'-a'-e" (see Appendix for the original violin version).

Even though the *frottole* and madrigal examples are presented here as solo pieces, the lira da braccio, in combination with an ensemble of instruments and voices, can be attractively used in instrumental introductions, accompaniments, and interludes between strophes to such pieces. That the lira da braccio was used in purely instrumental situations seems evident by the *Pasamezo* example in the Pesaro Ms., and by the reference to the instrument in Marini's *Capriccio.*

The repertoire selected here is intended mainly to show how such music can be adapted to fit the lira da braccio. With the help of the chords and fingering charts, it is hoped that further arrangements of repertoire can be facilitated. In the chart below numbers refer to open strings and fingerings; "t" refers to the use of the thumb, or the thumb nail against an off-the-fingerboard string. Additional signs indicate the following: ´ = sharp, ´´ = double sharp, ` = flat, `` = double flat, or their enharmonic equivalents (see also p. 57). For alto tuning see p. 118.

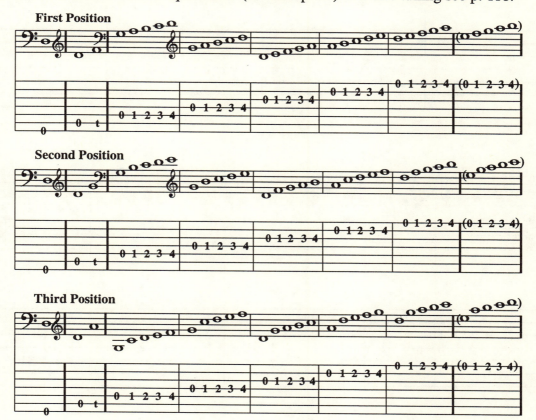

S'io sedo a l'ombra amor

Lira da braccio:

S.S.J. arrangement for lira da braccio
(Original: one tone lower)

Marco Cara

Petrucci, Libro V (1505)

Tuning

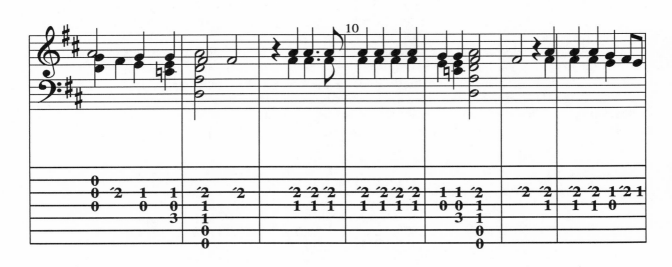

O felici occhi miei
(Il primo libro di Madrigali . . . , 1539)
S.S.J. arrangement for lira da braccio

Jacob Arcadelt

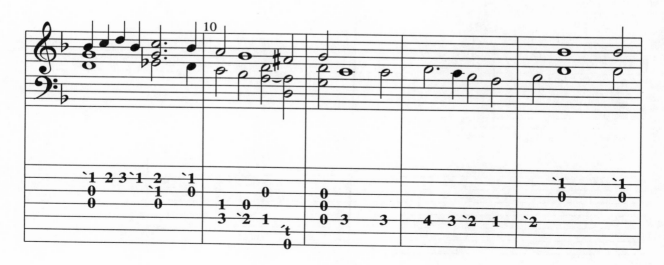

O felici occhi/Arcadelt

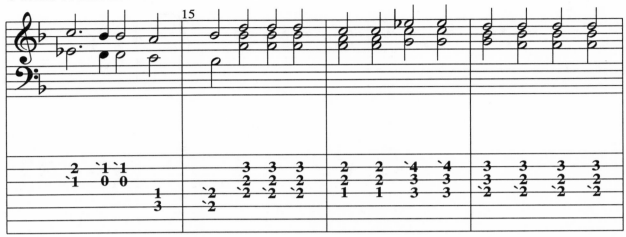

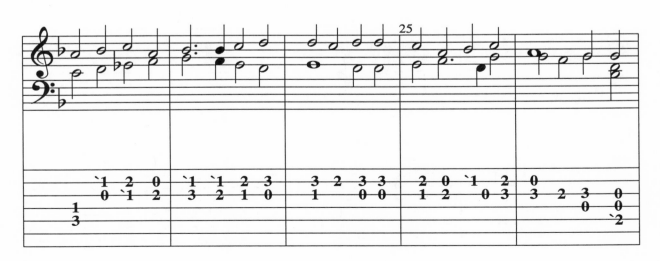

O felici occhi/Arcadelt

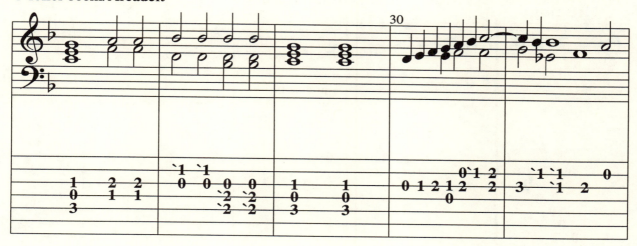

Con pianto e con dolore

Anon.

Lira da braccio:

S.S.J. arrangement for lira da braccio   Petrucci, Libro IV (1505)
(Original: fifth lower)

Tuning

Con pianto e con dolore/Anon.

Io non compro più speranza

Lira da braccio:

S.S.J. arrangement for lira da braccio
(Original: fourth lower)

Marco Cara
Petrucci, Libro I (1504)

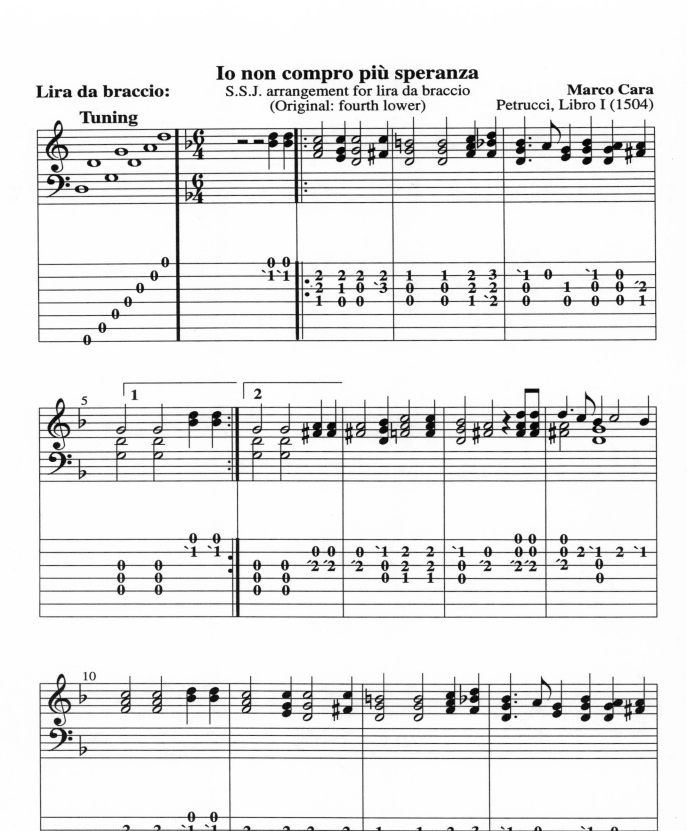

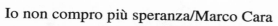
Io non compro più speranza/Marco Cara

Music to "Il Sacrificio" (Agostino Beccari 1554)

Lira da braccio: S.S.J. accompaniment for lira da braccio   **Alfonso della Viola**
(Original: whole tone lower)

Tu ch'ai le cor - na ri - guar - dan - ti ⌣ al cie - lo

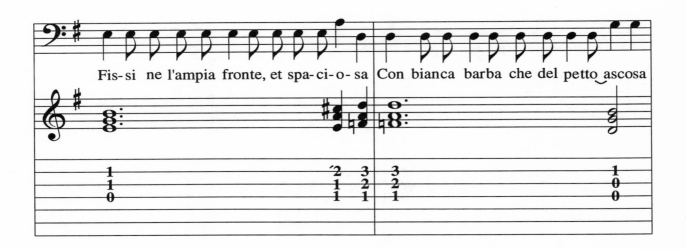

Fis- si ne l'ampia fronte, et spa- ci- o- sa   Con bianca barba che del petto ⌣ ascosa

Tien la parte maggior col lun- go pe- lo   Tu che'n ve- ce di ves- ta ⌣ o d'altro ve- lo

94

"Il Sacrificio"/Alfonso della Viola

Por - ti il gran cuoio cin-to | Di bel color di-pin-to | Et con macchie dis-tin-to

Che stu - por grande apport - ta | O' Pan Li - ce - o

2.

Tu che come ver Re lo scettro tieni
Ne l'una mano come celeste dono
Ne l'altra lo stromento onde quel suono
Sì dolce trahi ch'ogni empio cor affreni
Tu che con piè di capra vita meni
Con faccia di colore
Tra rosso e nero; il core
Mostrane il tuo favore
Tanto grato a ciascuno
O' Pan Liceo.

3.

Habbi del gregge e dell'armento cura
Che va pascendo in queste folte selve
Ove sta d'ogni intorno d'aspre belve
Stuol, che l'anci de et di nascosto'l fura
Guardalo ogni hor da incanto o' da fatura
Guardalo da ogni male
Poi che gli è tanto frale
Se'l pregar nostro sale
In sino a'le tue orechie
O' Pan Liceo.

* Einstein I, p. 301.

Chorus "Il Sacrificio"/Alfonso della Viola (Original: whole tone lower)

To be sung after verse 1.

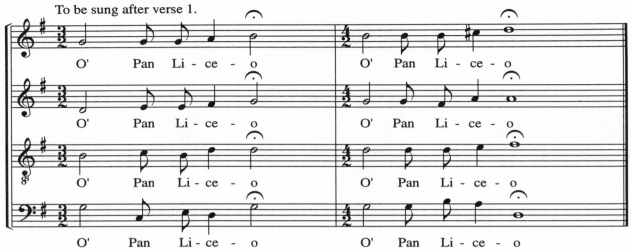

To be sung after verse 2.

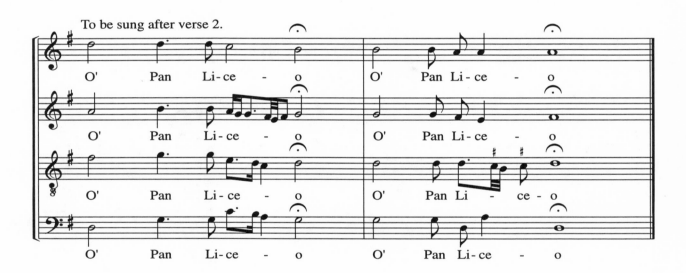

To be sung after verse 3.

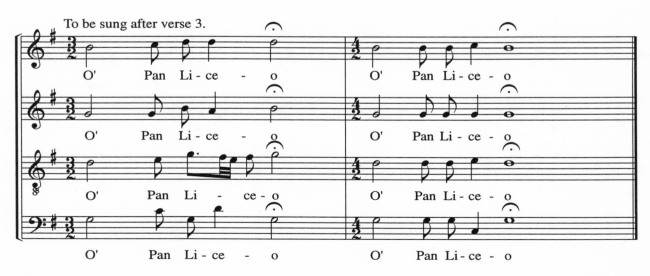

96

"Il Sacrificio"/Alfonso della Viola
S.S.J. accompaniments to verses 2 and 3.

Romanesca
(Passamezzo moderno)

Anon.
Pesaro Ms.

Lira da braccio:
Tuning

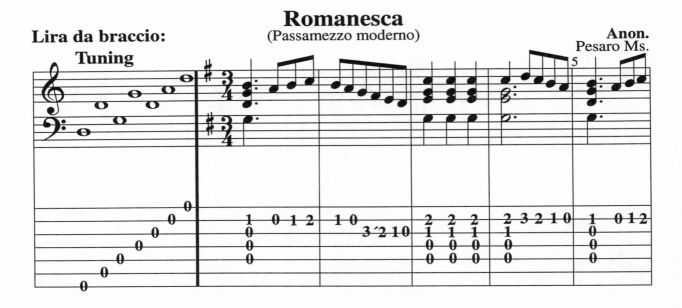

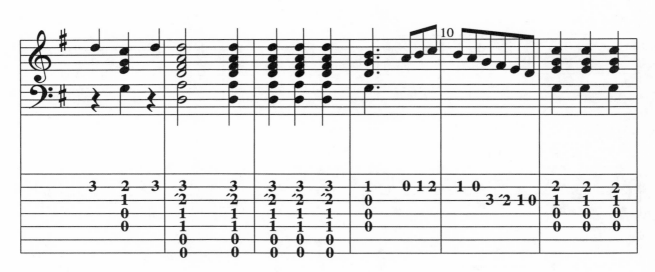

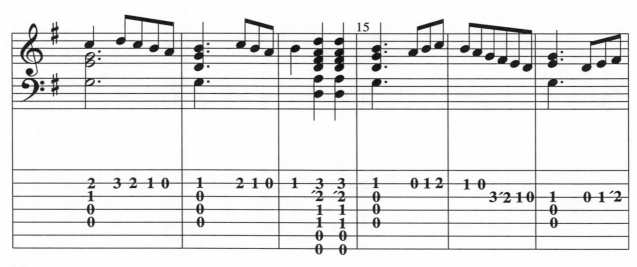

(Romanesca/Anon.)

Pasamezo de lira (fragment)

Aime sospiri

Lira da braccio: S.S.J. arrangement for alto lira da braccio (Escorial Ms.)

Aime sospiri

Lira da braccio: S.S.J. accompaniment for alto lira da braccio

Aime sospiri/Anon.

-gai mai sof-fri-re Que-ste'l do - lor che mi dif-fa - ce.

(Justiniani)   Petrucci, Frottole VI (1506)

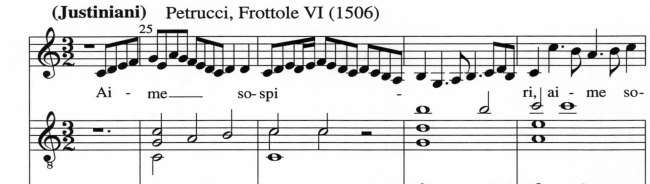

Ai - me____ so-spi ____ ri, ai - me so-

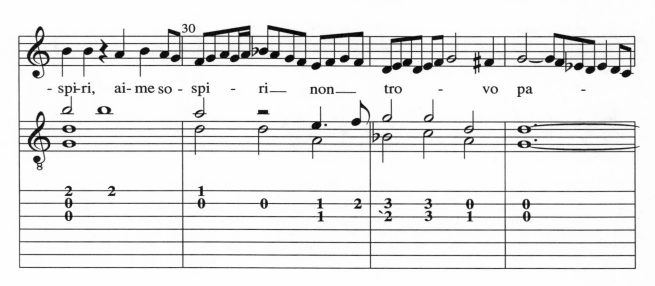

-spi-ri, ai-me so - spi - ri____ non____ tro - vo pa -

Aime sospiri/Anon.

Aime sospiri/Anon.

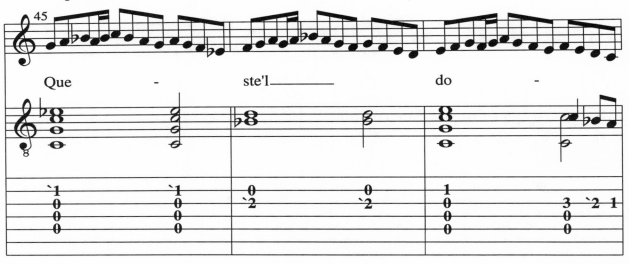

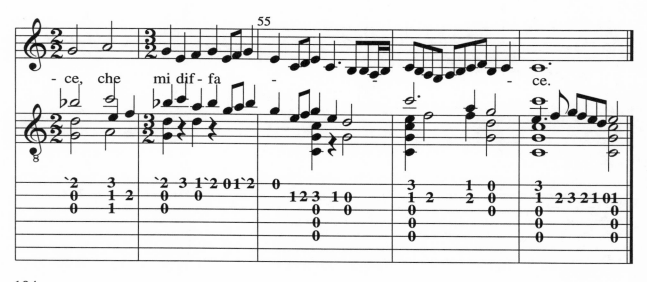

Capriccio

S.S.J. arrangement for lira da braccio

Lira da braccio:
Tuning

Biagio Marini
Venice, 1626

(Capriccio/Marini)

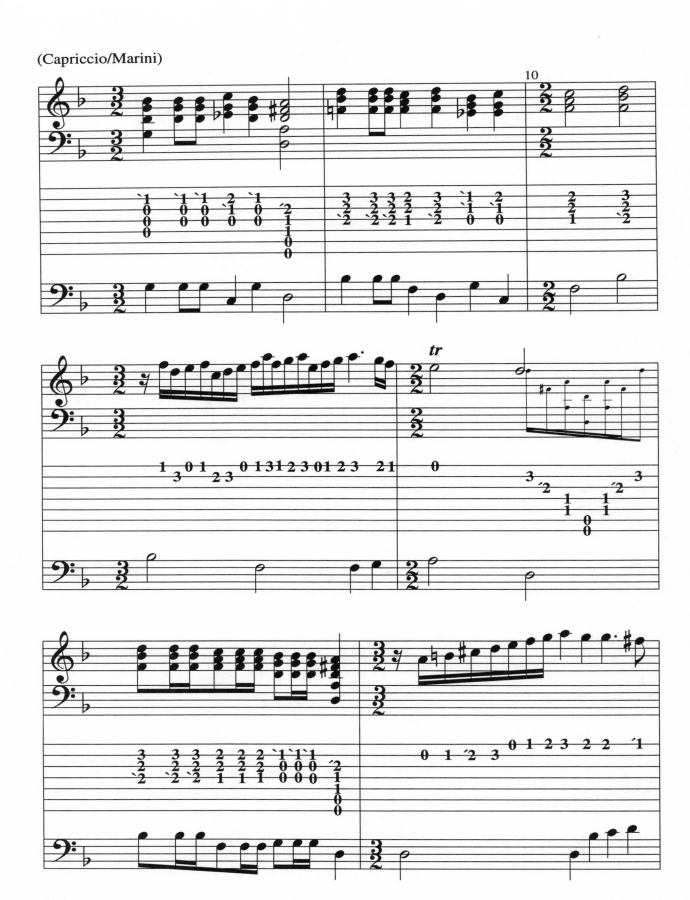

106

(Capriccio/Marini)

Appendix

Commentary

Some problems occur in transcribing the tablature of the Pesaro Ms. in the section *Tutte i tone de la lira* (see the Pesaro Ms. p. 176 facsimile on p. 112, and the transcription on p. 114). The "1" numbers shown on the strings off the fingerboard (d-d') are isolated by lines in the original which might indicate mistakes, as suggested by H. M. Brown ("Sixteenth-Century Instrumentation"). It has been documented, however, that such strings were stopped by means of a brass ring on the thumb (see C-18, where one string is stopped in this manner). If the "1" numbers indicate a placement relative to those strings on the fingerboard the pitches of f-f' result because of the longer string length of the two off-the-fingerboard strings, a result which would fit the remaining harmony of the chord. In the second such chord the unnumbered fourth string would have to be either stopped with the first finger along with the third string, producing the pitch "a," or jumped over with the bow.

The third, fifth, and seventh chords in the series present some problems as well, possibly mixing up the uses of "0" and "1" and reinforcing the idea that there are mistakes in the tablature. By exchanging some of these numbers Ivanoff (*Das Pesaro-Manuskript*) transcribes these chords with more logical harmonic solutions. The fact that four chords in the series (the fourth, ninth, eleventh, and twelfth) show one finger position for three strings seems to indicate that these strings were meant to be close together yet distant enough to allow them to be fingered separately, as seen in the third chord (provided the chord is not a mistake). On the other hand, a *barré* type fingering could execute chords where three strings require one fingering position by using two fingers, including the thumb. The accidentals in the transcription, not being precisely indicated in the original tablature, are applied to represent all the notes (*Tutte i tone de la lira*) of at least one octave.

The solmization and numbers, written by a different hand diagonally across the bottom of p. 175 of the Pesaro Ms., appear under the title *Aria Romana*. The example below is a possible interpretation of this table, revealing a chord pattern showing vague elements of the *Romanesca* and *Passamezzo moderno*. The solfège follows the lowest notes of the lira da braccio chords, and the numbers appear to be reminders for fingerings, all of which fit the chords. The + and # signs seem to indicate major, or raised thirds.

It is hoped that some day the missing pages (pp. 177-88) of the Pesaro Ms. will turn up. According to the manuscript index that would bring to light several more pieces: p. 177 *e(h) non* (or: *Darò*) *più guerra*, and on p. 184 *Bataglia* (see Ivanov, *Das Pesaro-Manuskript*, p. 116).

Marini states at the beginning of his *Capriccio* (see p. 116) that, of the three strings which according to the title play in the style of the lira, the two lowest should be close together. There is some indication that the two lowest fingered strings were sometimes placed closer together on liras da braccio, yet as seen in the Pesaro Ms. and the Marini piece they had to be separated enough to be fingered independently. The closeness (*vicine*) might refer to their proximity from the standpoint of bowing, that is, a flatter bridge.

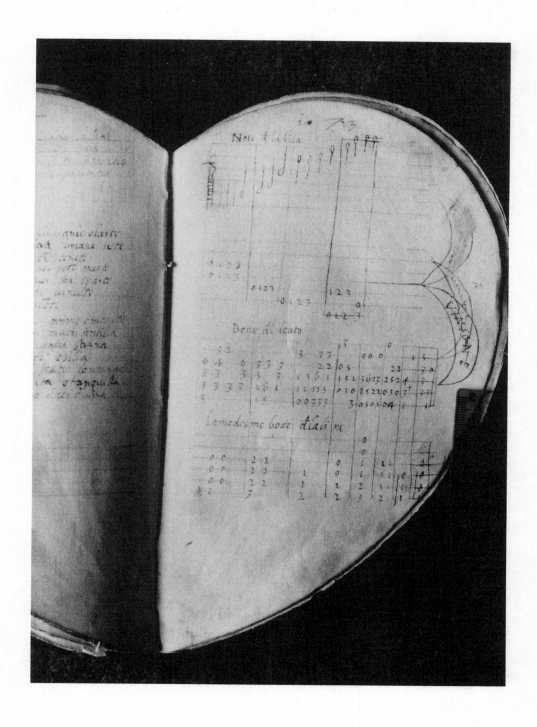

Pesaro Manuscript, Biblioteca Oliveriana, Ms. 1144, p. 173 (actual size)

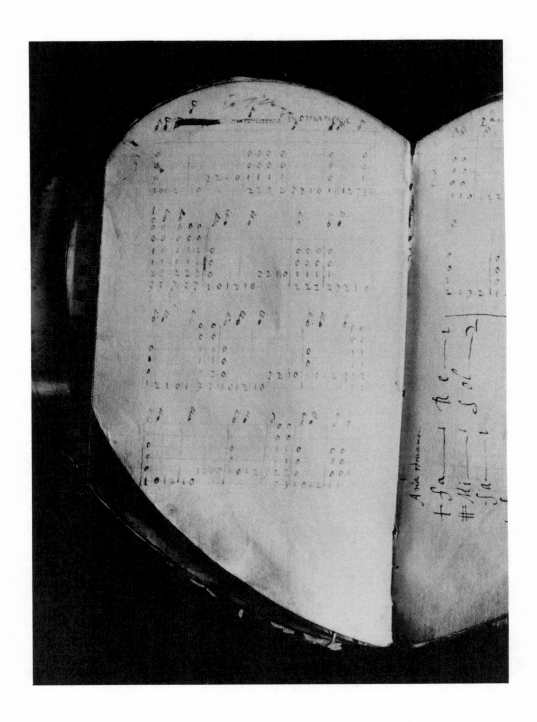

Pesaro Manuscript, Biblioteca Oliveriana, Ms. 1144, p. 174 (actual size)

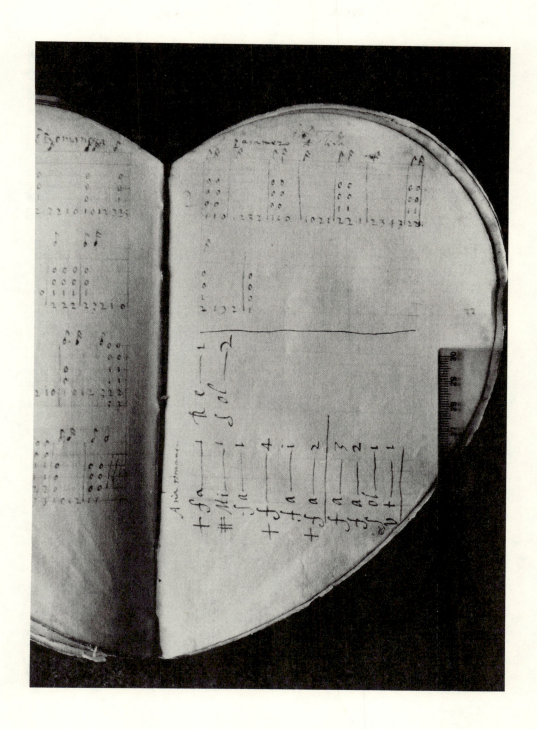

Pesaro Manuscript, Biblioteca Oliveriana, Ms. 1144, p. 175 (actual size)

Pesaro Manuscript, Biblioteca Oliveriana, Ms. 1144, p. 176 (actual size)

Romanesca
(Passamezzo moderno)

[Lira da braccio]

[Tuning]

Pasamezo de lira (fragment)

[Lira da braccio]
[Tuning]
Botte del leuto

Le medesme botte de la lira

[Tuning]
Note de la lira

Tutte i tone de la lira

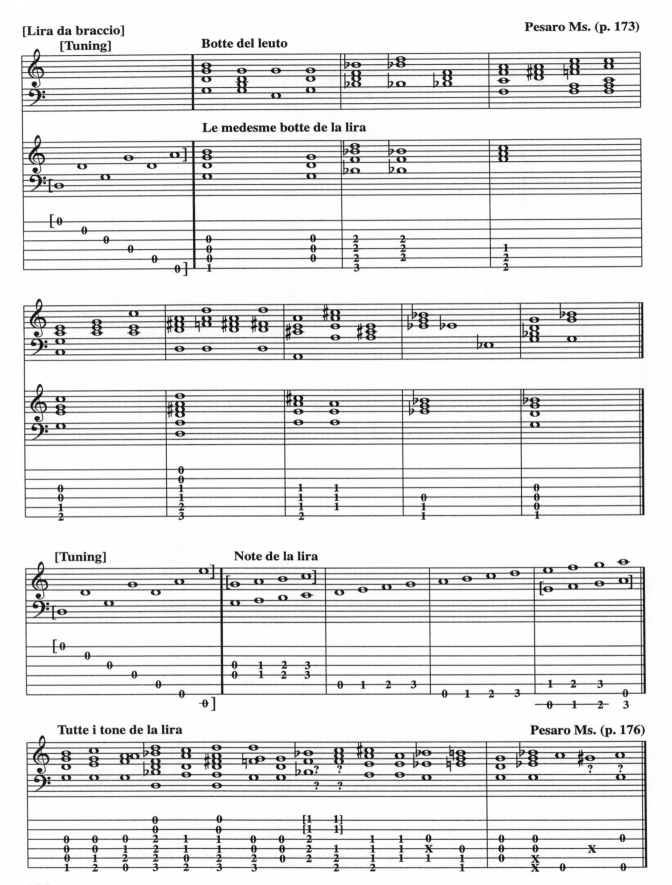

Ayme sospiri

Anon. (Escorial Ms. IV.a.24)

Ai - me so - spi - ri Ai - me so - spi - re Ai - me so -

spi - ri non tro - vo pa - ce che de - go fa - re

che de - go fa - re se non mo - ri - re E non po - tro O -

gai mai sof - fri - re Que ste'l do - lor che mi dif - fa - ce.

Capriccio Per Sonare il Violino con tre corde à modo di Lira

Biagio Marini
Venice, 1626

(Capriccio/Marini)

Fingering Chart for Alto Tuning

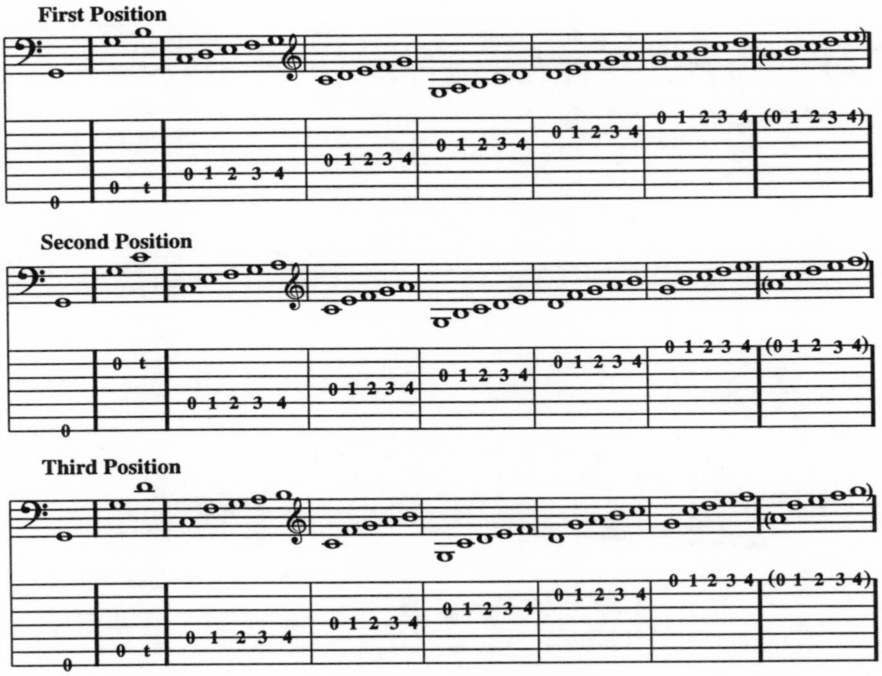

First Position

Second Position

Third Position

List of Instrument Makers

The following is a list of a few instrument makers who have already made liras da braccio, or who have expressed their interest in doing so.

Horst L. Kloss
1200 Great Plain Avenue
Needham, Massachusetts 02192
U.S.A.
Tel. 617/444-4383

Daniel Larson
26 N. 28th Avenue E
Duluth, Minnesota 55812
U.S.A.
Tel. 218/724-8011

John Pringle
2218 Mount Willing Road
Efland, North Carolina 27243
U.S.A.
Tel. Office: 919/563-4118.
Has made copies of both the Maria and the
Gasparo liras da braccio in Oxford.

Fabrizio Reginato
Fonte Alto
Via Paderno
Italy
Tel. 0039/423-58649
Has made copies of the Maria lira da braccio in
Oxford and the anonymous lira da braccio no.
1443 in Brussels

David T. Van Zandt
1119 N.W. 60th
Seattle, Washington 98107
U.S.A.
Tel. 206/789-7294

Bibliography

Abbiati, Franco. *Storia Della Musica.* Vol. I, *Dalle Origini A Cinquecento.* Milan: Garzanti, 1st ed. 1967, 2nd ed. 1974.

d'Alessi, G. "Maestri e Cantori Fiamminghi nella Cappella Musicale del Duomo di Treviso (1411-1561)." *Tijdschrift der Vereenigung voor Nederlandse Muziekgschiedenis* XV (1939): 147 ff.

Arte Cristiana, An International Review of Art History and Liturgical Arts, Vol. 737, March-April 1990; Vol. 741, November-December 1990.

Baines, Anthony. *European and American Musical Instruments.* London: Batsford Ltd., 1966.

Baines, Anthony. *Music Instruments through the Ages.* London: Penguin Books Ltd., 1961; reprint 1963, 1966.

Bertelli, Sergio. *Italian Renaissance Courts.* London: Sidgwick & Jackson, 1986.

Bessaraboff, Nicholas. *Ancient European Musical Instruments.* New York: October House, Inc., 1941, 1964.

Bosseur, Jean-Yves. *Musique passion d'artistes.* Geneva: Skira, 1991.

Bowles, Edmund A. *Musikgeschichte in Bildern.* Vol. III, *Musik des Mittelalters und der Renaissance,* Part 8. Leipzig: VEB Deutscher Verlag für Musik, 1977.

Boyden, David D. *Catalogue of the Hill Collection of Musical Instruments in the Ashmolean Museum.* Oxford and London: Oxford University Press, 1969; reprint 1970.

Boyden, David D. *The History of Violin Playing from Its Origins to 1761.* London: Oxford University Press, 1965; reprint 1967.

Brown, Howard Mayer. "Lira da braccio." *The New Grove Dictionary of Music and Musicians,* ed. Stanley Sadie. Vol. 11, 19-22.

Brown, Howard Mayer. "Sixteenth-Century Instrumentation: The Music for the Florentine Intermedii." Dallas: American Institute of Musicology, 1973, pp. 223-25.

Capri, Antonio. *Storia Della Musica, Dalle Antiche Civiltà Orientali Alla Musica Elettronica,* Vol. I, *Dalle Origini Al Cinquecento.* Milan: Casa Editrice Dr. Franscesco Vallardi, Società Editrice Libraria, 1st ed. 1969.

Clemencic, Réné. *Old Musical Instruments.* London: Weidenfeld and Nicolson, 1968.

Coover, James. *Musical Instrument Collections, Catalogues and Cognate Literature.* No. 47 of Detroit Studies in Music Bibliography. General Editor, Bruno Nettl. Detroit: Information Coordinators, Inc., 1981.

Disertori, Benvenuto. "L'Arciviolatalira in un quadro del Secento." *Rivista Musicale Italiana* (RMI) 44 (1940): 199-211.

Disertori, Benvenuto. *Le Frottole,* Vol. I. Cremona: Athenaeum Cremonense, 1954.

Disertori, Benvenuto. *Le Frottole per Canto e Liuto Intabulate da Franciscus Bossinensis.* Milan: G. Ricordi, 1964.

Disertori, Benvenuto. "Pratica e tecnica della lira da braccio." *Rivista Musicale Italiana* (RMI) 45 (1941): 150-75.

Einstein, Alfred. *The Italian Madrigal,* Vol. I. Princeton: Princeton University Press, 1949.

Encyclopedia of World Art, Vol. XII. New York, Toronto, and London: McGraw-Hill, 1966.

Prince d'Essling. *Les Livres à figures venetiens de la fin du XVe siècle au commencement du XVIe.* Florence and Paris: 1907-1914.

Francia, Mons. Ennio. *Pinacoteca Vaticana.* Milan: Aldo Martello Editore, 1960.

Geiser, Brigitte. *Studien zur Frühgeschichte der Violine.* Bern and Stuttgart: Paul Haupt, 1974.

Haas, Robert. "Aufführungspraxis der Musik," in *Handbuch der Musikwissenschaft.* Potsdam: Akademische Verlagsgesellschaft Athenaion M.B.H., 1934.

Hajdecki, Alexander. *Die Italienische Lira da Braccio, Eine Kunsthistorische Studie zur Geschichte der Violine.* Mastar, 1892; Amsterdam: Municipal Museum of the Hague, 1965.

Haraszti, Emile. "La Technique des Improvisateurs de Langue Vulgaire et de Latin au Quatrocento." *Revue Belge de Musicologie,* Vol. IX (1955): 12-31.

Heydenreich, Ludwig H., and Passavant, Günter. *Universum der Kunst, Italienische Renaissance, Die Grossen Meister 1500-1540.* Munich: C. H. Beck, 1975.

Hind, Arthur Mayer. *Early Italian Engraving.* London: 1938-1948.

Hayes, Gerald R. *Musical Instruments and Their Music, 1500-1750.* Vol. II, *The Viols, and Other Bowed Instruments.* Oxford: Oxford University Press, 1930.

Ivanoff, Vladimir. *Das Pesaro-Manuskript, Ein Beitrag zur Frühgeschichte der Lautentabulatur.* Tutzing: Hans Schneider, 1988.

Ivanoff, Vladimir. *Eine Zentrale Quelle der Frühen Italienischen Lautenpraxis, Edition der Handschrift Pesaro, Biblioteca Oliveriana, Ms. 1144.* Tutzing: Hans Schneider, 1988.

Kinsky, Georg. *Geschichte der Musik in Bildern.* Leipzig: Breitkopf & Härtel, 1929.

Kinsky, Georg. *Musikhistorisches Museum von W. Heyer in Cöln,* Vol. II, *Katalog.* Leipzig: Breitkopf & Härtel, 1912.

Lützeler, Heinrich. *Musik.* Freiburg in Breisgau: Verlag Herder, 1943.

Mahillon, Victor Charles. *Catalogue descriptif et analytique du Musée Instrumental du Conservatoire de Musique de Bruxelles,* Vol. III. Ghent, 1900.

Monical, William L. *Shapes of the Baroque: The Historical Development of Bowed String Instruments.* Philadelphia: Smith-Edwards-Dunlap Co., 1989.

Moreck, Curt. *Die Musik in der Malerei.* Munich: G. Hirth, 1924.

Munrow, David. *Instruments of the Middle Ages and Renaissance.* London: Oxford University Press, 1976. *Musikinstrumente des Mittelalters und der Renaissnce.* Celle: Moeck, 1980.

Osthoff, Wolfgang. *Theatergesang und darstellende Musik in der italienischen Renaissance.* 2 vols. Tutzing: Hans Schneider, 1969.

Otto, Irmgard, and Adelmann, Olga. *Katalog der Streichinstrumente,* Staatliches Institut für Musikforschung, Preussischer Kulturbesitz, Musikinstrumenten-Museum Berlin. Berlin: 1975.

Parson, Priscilla. "An Organological Study of Leg-Held Bowed Chordophones." Diss., University of Wisconsin, 1989.

La Pittura in Italia. Vol. I. *Il Cinquecento.* Milan: Electa, 1987-1988.

Pope-Hennessy, John. *Renaissance Bronzes from the Samuel H. Kress Collection.* London, 1965

Ravenel, Bernard. "Rebec und Fiedel--Ikonographie und Spielweise." *Basler Jahrbuch für Historische Musikpraxis* VIII (1984): 105-30.

Remnant, Mary. *Musical Instruments of the West.* New York: St. Martin's Press, 1978.

Rubsamen, Walter H. "The Earliest French Lute Tablature." *Journal of the American Musicological Society* XXI/3, (1968): 286-99.

Rühlmann, Julius. *Die Geschichte der Bogeninstrumente.* Braunschweig: Friedrich Vieweg und Sohn, 1882.

Sachs, Curt. *Sammlung alter Musikinstrumente bei der Staatliche Hochschule für Musik zu Berlin.* Berlin, 1920.

Sander, Max. *Le Livre à figures italien.* Milan, 1942.

Sauerlandt, Max. *Die Musik in Fünf Jahrhunderten der Europäischen Malerei.* Leipzig: Karl Robert Langewiesche Verlag, 1922.

Schlosser, Julius von. *Die Sammlung alter Musikinstrumente,* Vol. 3. Vienna: A. Schroll and Co., 1920.

Spicer, Simon. *The Shrine to Music Museum.* Santa Barbara: Companion Press, 1988.

Stauder, Wilhelm. *Alte Musiknstrumente in ihrer vieltausendjährigen Entwicklung und Geschichte.* Braunschweig: Klinkhardt and Biermann, 1973.

Winternitz, Emanuel. *Leonardo da Vinci as a Musician.* New Haven and London: Yale University Press, 1982.

Winternitz, Emanuel. "Lira da braccio." *Die Musik in Geschichte und Gegenwart* (MGG), Vol. 8. Kassel: Bärenreiter, 1960, pp. 935-54.

Winternitz, Emanuel. *Musical Instruments and Their Symbolism in Western Art.* New Haven and London: Yale University Press, 1979.

Winternitz, Emanuel. *Musical Instruments of the Western World*. New York and Toronto: McGraw-Hill, n. d.

Witten, Laurence II. "Apollo, Orpheus, and David: a Study of the Crucial Century in the Development of Bowed Strings in North Italy, 1480-1580." *Journal of the American Musical Instrument Society* (JAMIS) 1 (1975): 5-55.

Woodfield, Ian. *The Early History of the Viol*. Cambridge: Cambridge University Press, 1984.

Apollo, in Ovid's, *Metamorphoses*, Venice, 1497.
(See A-1, p. 16)

Sterling Scott Jones received his musical training at the University of Wisconsin, the University of Illinois, Heidelberg University, and the Ecole Normale de Musique. He was a founding member of the Studio der frühen Musik and performed with this ensemble for eighteen years. He resides in Munich, Germany, and performs on early bowed string instruments with various groups.